NEW DIRECTIONS FOR ADULT AND (

D1440796

Ralph G. Brockett, *University of Tennessee, Knoxville*
EDITOR-IN-CHIEF

Alan B. Knox, *University of Wisconsin, Madison*
CONSULTING EDITOR

# Learn Deve

Lorraine
*Rutgers U*

Angela S
*Trenton S*

EDITORS

Number 53

JOSSEY-BA
San Franci

3-93

#26146838

LEARNING FOR PERSONAL DEVELOPMENT
*Lorraine A. Cavaliere, Angela Sgroi* (eds.)
New Directions for Adult and Continuing Education, no. 53
*Ralph G. Brockett,* Editor-in-Chief
*Alan B. Knox,* Consulting Editor

Microfilm copies of issues and articles are available in 16mm and 35mm, as well as microfiche in 105mm, through University Microfilms Inc., 300 North Zeeb Road, Ann Arbor, Michigan 48106.

LC 85-644750          ISSN 0195-2242          ISBN 1-55542-747-2

NEW DIRECTIONS FOR ADULT AND CONTINUING EDUCATION is part of The Jossey-Bass Higher and Adult Education Series and is published quarterly by Jossey-Bass Inc., Publishers, 350 Sansome Street, San Francisco, California 94104-1310 (publication number USPS 493-930). Second-class postage paid at San Francisco, California, and at additional mailing offices. POSTMASTER: Send address changes to New Directions for Adult and Continuing Education, Jossey-Bass Inc., Publishers, 350 Sansome Street, San Francisco, California 94104-1310.

SUBSCRIPTIONS for 1992 cost $45.00 for individuals and $60.00 for institutions, agencies, and libraries.

EDITORIAL CORRESPONDENCE should be sent to the Editor-in-Chief, Ralph G. Brockett, Dept. of Technological and Adult Education, University of Tennessee, 402 Claxton Addition, Knoxville, Tennessee 37996-3400.

Cover photograph by Wernher Krutein/PHOTOVAULT © 1990.

 The paper used in this journal is acid-free and meets the strictest guidelines in the United States for recycled paper (50 percent recycled waste, including 10 percent postconsumer waste). Manufactured in the United States of America.

# CONTENTS

# Editors' Notes

Success is often best achieved by modeling similar success elsewhere. What better way for adult and continuing educators to learn how to foster highly charged, exciting, and productive learning situations than to find where they are already occurring, analyze them, and adapt their critical elements to other learning contexts?

Numerous adult educators who have attended presentations of our research (Cavaliere studied the learning behaviors used by the Wright brothers that led to the invention of the airplane, and Sgroi examined adult learning in modern dance) have suggested that we try to find a way to "bottle" their excitement and quality of learning. We have accepted the challenge.

This volume is a robust collection of experiences, contexts, knowledge, and insights, which, though not comprehensive, suggests the range of the issue. Based on our own experience, our assumption is that some of the most engaging learning is that undertaken for personal development.

Although quite varied, every chapter has the learner as a common focus: what happens *inside* the individual rather than within groups or the larger society (even though some of the discussions include a look at the individual within the larger society) and what the action of the learner consists of. The assumption of each author is that learning is dynamic; therefore, it is constantly changing and moving. Each discussion begins with that perspective and, as a result, yields some startling insights.

The chapters are organized so that they move from the conceptual to the case study, and from examples of personal learning in particular settings and contexts to practical applications. The first chapter is a theoretical overview of the phenomenon of learning for personal development as seen by major educators, psychologists, and philosophers. It focuses the issue, defines the volume's limits, and identifies theoretical frameworks that inform this work.

In Chapter Two, Ellen J. Langer and Justin Pugh Brown describe mindful learning and, in doing so, foreshadow some themes that continue to emerge in a variety of ways in the later chapters. *Mindfulness* is a phenomenon in which the mind is attending to the present moment. In this state, the mind maintains a healthy degree of uncertainty and continually categorizes and recategorizes, labels and relabels the world—a process that yields new perspectives and creates new options for the individual. Possible applications for teaching and learning are also discussed.

David Carr, in Chapter Three, describes cultural institutions as "agencies in their cultures," designed to evoke cognitive transformations. He states that "they sustain situations and processes for the resolution of unknowns in the lives of learners. . . ." Although Carr's work emphasizes learning in cultural institutions, it also provides both a theoretical base and practical method of approach that can inform educators in any setting.

In Chapter Four, Robert L. Williams explains that "action learning often challenges existing rules, experiments with truth, questions the efficacy of mediating institutions, and leads to significant personal and social change." His discussion derives from case studies of a number of ordinary people who achieved national prominence as social advocates.

The case study approach is continued in Chapter Five, where Lorraine A. Cavaliere examines the independent learning processes used by the Wright brothers in inventing the airplane. She has developed a learning process model that illustrates the "function and nature of learning during the inventive process."

"Learning in the arts differs from learning in other areas in some significant ways," according to Angela Sgroi, author of Chapter Six. Sgroi illustrates learning for personal development as it proceeds in a modern dance studio. She argues that the development of intuitive knowledge, a nonverbal means of communication, and its process orientation serve the learner in all aspects of life.

In Chapter Seven, Mary Alice Wolf suggests that the study of personal development would benefit from a look at older learners, the most concentrated cohort of people to engage in that type of activity. With retirement and diminished family responsibilities, many people are finally free to engage wholeheartedly in personal development.

Leonard P. Oliver's discussion of study circles, Chapter Eight, begins the volume's movement toward providing mechanisms for the application and institutionalization of ideas. He provides specific guidelines for formulating a purpose for, creating, and conducting study circles.

Learning in liberal studies, claims L. Steven Zwerling in Chapter Nine, offers a base of information about the world; more importantly, it develops skills—"portable skills"—and a process for learning how to learn, solve problems, and generally survive in the modern world. These skills foster success in all contexts of adult life, including the workplace. And even when a liberal course or curriculum is directed to developing employee skill, the real value of the learning is that those skills enhance the development of the individual. Zwerling takes the discussion a step further by recommending specific ways that this form of personal development can be implemented.

In Chapter Ten, we conclude the volume with observations summarizing the elements of learning for personal development presented by the contributors. The chapter makes suggestions to adult educators that represent a synthesis of the ideas presented throughout the book.

Part of the excitement in editing a work of this type is watching it develop its own character, style, and form. Though the authors were asked to participate because of the similarity of their work to the volume's theme, it is their different approaches and perspectives that are illuminating.

We hope that you will benefit—as we did—from the considerable experience and knowledge of these authors. One of the virtues they seem to share is that they do not put education and learning into boxes. They see them within the context of an individual's whole life and as interwoven with everything from daily struggles in the home or office to spiritual and broad reflections on life itself.

Angela Sgroi
Lorraine A. Cavaliere
Editors

*ANGELA SGROI is executive assistant to the vice president for academic affairs at Trenton State College, New Jersey.*

*LORRAINE A. CAVALIERE is director of continuing studies at Rutgers University.*

*Learning that leads to personal development and social change is highly interactive and does not occur in isolation. These interactions between the learner and the context form a learning system that reflects the power of active learning.*

# Active Learning: Perspectives on Learning That Leads to Personal Development and Social Change

*Lorraine A. Cavaliere, Angela Sgroi*

"A mind that is stretched to a new idea never returns to its original dimensions."

—Oliver Wendell Holmes

We humans seem to continually stretch to new ideas, sometimes in spite of ourselves. Because this volume is concerned with the kind of learning that individuals engage in primarily for personal reasons, we explore the paths followed by learners who have problems to solve, goals to accomplish, and dreams to fulfill. Each chapter provides a perspective on the nature of this kind of active, dynamic learning that significantly changes the individual and, sometimes, society at large.

After comparing the results of our own diverse research, we consulted other researchers and practitioners in adult education, psychology, library science, gerontology, and sociology whose work focused on issues of personal learning. We discovered striking identifiable characteristics and patterns that you will see in the chapters that follow. During the course of learning for personal development, the learner experiences cognitive and psychological discoveries that escalate the learning and bring about personal transformations and knowledge revolutions.

The purpose of this chapter is to review briefly the work of some of the major writers and thinkers whose ideas provide insights into learning for personal development. In our attempt to describe the qualities of this

NEW DIRECTIONS FOR ADULT AND CONTINUING EDUCATION, no. 53, Spring 1992 © Jossey-Bass Publishers

phenomenon, we examined learning for personal development in three ways: the self, the context, and the learning system formed by the interaction between the two.

## The Self

Our analysis of the self involves a description of the internal traits and manifest behaviors exhibited by the learner. We focus on the internal forces or qualities that motivate and attract the learner to the particular learning activities undertaken for personal development, the qualities adult learners generally bring to most of these activities, and the results of that attraction. The individuals analyzed in this volume take action. Their activity gains momentum and spurs them on to reach goals that they set for themselves during the earlier stages of their learning journeys. Intense feelings—passion, desire, and even affliction—drive these individuals to devise and identify strategies and tools to assist them in their learning. Patience, determination, and curiosity seem to be qualities that reap success for these learners, and their successes (and failures) act as feedback and motivation for them to continue on. These individuals are students of life; they extend themselves, explore, and take risks in ways that bring about dissonance as well as discovery.

## The Learning Context

A myriad of variables compose the contexts fostering this type of active learning and providing information and resources to learners that make their journey productive and successful. These contexts are charged with energy, ideas, and stimulation on the one hand and incongruencies and problems on the other; they present learners with opportunities for change, growth, and personal development.

Context is considered, in the broadest sense, to mean anything external to the learners, including local setting; historical context; cultural and social world views; values, behaviors, and standards; availability of resources; information; people; and the significance of timing to the learning process. The multifaceted nature of the context presents opportunities for the learner to garner layers of information and stimulus at varying intervals depending on individual readiness. The learner requires freedom and time to explore, study, contemplate, and question the elements in the environment.

## The Learning System

The learner is never separate and distinct from the context. If the universe of learning consists of the individual and the environment within which the individual functions, then the variables that should be examined are the characteristics of the learner and those of the context. The interaction between these two variables can be described as the nature of learning, and the outcomes of this learning are the (describable) impact that it has on these variables.

The learner and the context form a system. And it is the dynamic of this system that holds the fascination for the researcher. What are the behavioral processes and patterns that exemplify learning? What elements in the context facilitate learning? How can we as researchers and practitioners use this information further to understand and implement learning?

## The Active Nature of Learning

One common element that characterizes learning for personal development is action. John Dewey (1938) and William James (in Elias and Merriam, 1980) maintain that knowledge is subordinate to action. The meaning and truth of ideas are determined by their relation to practice. It is the essence of action that delineates the learning that follows.

Action begets learning, and learning begets change. Active learning involves the dynamic interchange between characteristics of the learner and characteristics in the context. This type of active, dynamic operative learning can occur within an infinite number of contexts and scenarios.

Personal development that results from this type of learning involves metamorphosis: the learner can never be the same as before the learning experience. This metamorphic nature of learning seems to be a dynamic state whereby energy is released that engages the organism to begin a stage of discountenance that leads to evolution. The stage of discountenance experienced by the learner provides an optimal opportunity for transformative learning; it is usually triggered by a situation that is highly emotional and meaningful to the learner and that motivates an individual to undertake active learning in order to achieve homeostasis. This process is similar to Vygotsky's (1978) theory of the zone of proximal development, the equilibration of Piaget as reinforced by Williams (1989), and Csikszentmihalyi's (1982) zone for optimal flow (a zone between frustration and boredom). As learning gains momentum (usually due to the learner's successful accomplishments), stages of action occur that result in total revolution of being and thought.

Gibbons (1990) proposes that there are three kinds of learning: natural, formal, and personal. Natural learning is interactive; the individual interacts spontaneously with the environment while the content for learning is selected from what is available in the environment. The method of instruction is transactional, a process that occurs between accidental influence and inner state. Formal learning is directed for the individual through a prescribed, systematic learning procedure, with the content being assigned by an educational authority. Personal learning is self-initiated, and the individual designs the desired learning procedure. The content is selected and organized by the learner, who in turn enacts and monitors his or her own learning procedure.

The type of learning we are exploring seems to be a combination of natural, formal, and personal learning as described by Gibbons. Even though we are using the label "learning for personal development," it does not fit the schemata as described by Gibbons. The type of learning we are examining occurs in formal as well as informal settings, and the learners, regardless of the context, are actively involved in their learning. That action is the common element that permeates the process.

The nature of the adult learning described in this text seems to have broader parameters than the self-directed learning as described by Knowles, Tough, Brookfield, and Candy (in Merriam and Caffarella, 1991; Brockett and Hiemstra, 1991), although Candy (1991) comes closest with his description of autodidacticism. The authors in this book describe learning that is active, problem-centered, goal-oriented, cyclical, and interactive. The topics examined by the authors reveal that the learner, in every instance, is actively involved in the learning process: cognitively, physically, and emotionally. Physically taking some form of action is the most powerful aspect of initiating learning. Physical involvement, motivated by high emotional commitment, drives the learner through the context in an exploratory fashion whereby each subsequent learning behavior is a result of its antecedent.

## Humanistic Origins

The type of learning being explored in this text appears to pervade the major learning theories. The learners being analyzed respond to stimuli and feedback that result in behavioral changes (behaviorist); they rely on internal cognitive structuring, information processing, and perception to learn (cognitivist); they are involved in interactions with others and the environment as an integral part of their learning (social learning); and the individual is fully engaged, cognitively and affectively, in fulfilling personal potential (humanist) (Merriam and Caffarella, 1991).

However, the roots of this type of active, self-directed learning do have qualities that traditionally stem from a predominantly humanistic perspective. Aristotle defined an approach to living that reflects the nature of this active learning. In *Nicomachean Ethics*, he discusses *eudaimonia*, a philosophical system that expects individuals to recognize and live in accordance with their daimon (or "true self") as a guide to selecting activities for personal expression and fulfillment. Carl Gustave Jung (1968) espoused the process of *individuation*, the path to psychological and physiological integration and development. Abraham Maslow (1954), one of the major theoreticians of the humanist psychology movement in America, defined a hierarchy of human needs that has as its apex *self-actualization,* the need to fulfill one's potential. Closely related to Maslow's self-actualizing human being is the "fully functioning person" described by Carl Rogers (1969). He characterized the process of learning as a continuum of meaning ranging from meaningless memorizing to significant experiential learning. According to Rogers, experiential learning that fostered fully functioning individuals consisted of behaviors that involved the affective and cognitive modes, and the learning was self-initiated and evaluated by the individual. "In addition to Rogers and Maslow, scholars such as Buhler, Allport, Fromm, Sullivan, G. H. Mead, Frankl, May, Adler, Lewin, and Jourard have made significant contributions to the humanistic approach to adult learning" (Darkenwald and Merriam, 1982, p. 83).

Although the tradition of liberal education has used a teacher-centered methodology that seems to contradict the principles of humanistic learning theory, we see strong similarities in the goals of each, especially when more student-centered methodologies are used. Robert Hutchins and Mortimer Adler were the chief proponents of liberal education as a lifelong endeavor: "to be truly educated is a state achieved by self-direction, usually long after schooling is completed" (Langenbach, 1988, p. 56). The Great Books discussion programs and the Paideia proposal share the goal of promoting liberal education and have learning by doing and the development of the self as their philosophical bases. The Chatauqua movement is another example of adult education as a humanistic, liberal effort that promotes the personal development of individuals through experiences with multiple disciplines in the arts and sciences. The traditions of adult education have proven that education is not just for the elite, and the learners depicted in this text illustrate that a liberal education can be available to all in society willing to actively pursue their own learning.

Humanistic learning theorists directly influenced the practice of adult education. John Dewey's notion of learning by doing established a methodology for instruction that continues to frame educational practice (1938). Carl Weinberg's (1972) principles of humanistic psychology are closely aligned to the characteristics exhibited by the learners in this book: individuals learn in a free environment, learn by relating the world to their experiences (Dewey, 1938), learn cooperatively and from the inside out, and learn in relation to their human qualities (Darkenwald and Merriam, 1982). Paulo Freire (1968) exemplified the tradition of transformative learning as empowering the masses through acquisition of basic skills and knowledge. Knowles's (1980) principles of andragogy reflect the principles of humanistic philosophers and educators. Mezirow's (1991) theory of perspective transformation elegantly depicts the revolutionary nature of active learning.

This active nature of learning is the essence of the scenarios described in this book. So let us examine with our authors the nature of this experience and the energy unleashed when the learner springs into motion.

## References

Brockett, R. G., and Hiemstra, R. *Self-Direction in Adult Learning: Perspectives on Theory, Research, and Practice.* London and New York: Routledge, 1991.

Candy, P. C. *Self-Direction for Lifelong Learning: A Comprehensive Guide to Theory and Practice.* San Francisco: Jossey-Bass, 1991.

Csikszentmihalyi, M. *Flow: The Psychology of Optimal Experience.* New York: HarperCollins, 1982.

Darkenwald, G., and Merriam, S. *Adult Education: Foundations of Practice.* New York: Harper-Collins, 1982.

Dewey, J. *Experience and Education.* New York: Macmillan, 1938.

Elias, J., and Merriam, S. *Philosophical Foundations of Adult Education.* Malabar, Fla.: Krieger, 1980.

Freire, P. *Pedagogy of the Oppressed.* New York: Seabury Press, 1968.

Gibbons, M. "A Working Model of the Learning-How-to-Learn Process." In R. M. Smith and Associates, *Learning to Learn Across the Life Span.* San Francisco: Jossey-Bass, 1990.

Jung, C. G. *Analytical Psychology: Its Theory and Practice.* New York: Vintage Books, 1968.

Knowles, M. *The Modern Practice of Adult Education.* (Rev. ed.) Chicago: Follett, 1980.

Langenbach, M. *Curriculum Models in Education.* Malabar, Fla.: Krieger, 1988.

Maslow, A. *Hierarchy, Motivation, and Personality.* New York: HarperCollins, 1954.

Merriam, S. B., and Caffarella, R. S. *Learning in Adulthood: A Comprehensive Guide.* San Francisco: Jossey-Bass, 1991.

Mezirow, J. *Transformative Dimensions of Adult Learning.* San Francisco: Jossey-Bass, 1991.

Rogers, C. R. *Freedom to Learn.* Westerville, Ohio: Merrill, 1969.

Vygotsky, L. S. *Mind in Society: The Development of Higher Psychological Processes.* Cambridge, Mass.: Harvard University Press, 1978.

Weinberg, C. (ed.). *Humanistic Foundations of Education.* Englewood Cliffs, N.J.: Prentice Hall, 1972.

Williams, R. L. "Finding Voice: The Transition from Individualism to Social Advocacy." Unpublished doctoral dissertation, Fielding Institute, 1989.

LORRAINE A. CAVALIERE *is director of continuing studies at Rutgers University.*

ANGELA SGROI *is executive assistant to the vice president for academic affairs at Trenton State College, New Jersey.*

*Emphasizing understanding the power of uncertainty, acknowl-
edging the ambiguity of all human endeavors, and viewing failure
in a new context, the phenomenon here called* mindfulness
*foreshadows themes that emerge from each of the following
chapters.*

# Mindful Learning:
# A World Without Losers

*Ellen J. Langer, Justin Pugh Brown*

We live in a world where change is constantly present. We are continually
exhorted to try out new methods, to buy new educational products, to
learn new technologies, and to adopt different ways of looking or even
being. Observation tells us that some people can accept these changes
quite easily. They are the lucky ones. They move about amidst the seeming
upheavals as though they were the normal course of action or even an
opportunity.

For the rest of us, change is often stressful and difficult. What would
it take to become one of those people for whom change represents opportunity rather than dread? We might hope that education would enhance
our ability to perceive change as positive. Yet all too often the emphasis
placed on outcomes in our educational system prevents us from seeing
education as a process that is never finished. Outfitted with facts and
cognitive skills, the educated person generally is viewed as better equipped
for life than the person who lacks these valuable commodities. What does
it mean to think of education as a commodity? How confident can we be
that our newly learned facts are stable possessions (Ableson, 1986)? Does
education that is obtained so that we can compare favorably with others or
separate ourselves from those with less ability really prepare us for a changing world?

The purpose of this chapter is to examine the concept of mindfulness,
to investigate how it contributes to personal development and successful
living, and to consider how it might be incorporated into educational
settings.

NEW DIRECTIONS FOR ADULT AND CONTINUING EDUCATION, no. 53, Spring 1992 ©Jossey-Bass Publishers

## Mindfulness

The phenomenon we have come to call *mindfulness* (Langer, 1989) has led us to recognize that, although change occurs all of the time, we typically only notice it when it is big enough to break up our comfortable routines. Our *mindlessness* prevents us from seeing the smaller changes that provide the clues of what is to come. For example, our spouse may inform us that divorce has become an attractive idea, and the information may hit like a steel balloon, forcing us to notice that things are not as they were. But changes like these do not just happen; we just have to be open to see them.

Our understanding of mindfulness begins with an understanding of mindlessness and the ways we unwittingly trap ourselves. We experience the world and ourselves in it by making categories and creating distinctions among them. "He's the boss now," "She's a winner," "That's not the way to do it," "The white orchids are endangered," "This is a Chinese, not a Japanese, vase." Without categories, the world might escape us. Yet when we too rigidly rely on preformulated distinctions created in the past, we may forget that they are of our own making, and as such they may entrap us and freeze our thinking. Even the way a minor detail can feel wrong (like the reference above to a steel, rather than a lead, balloon) suggests how limiting these categories may be.

As described in *Mindfulness* (1989), Langer's grandmother had a brain tumor that ultimately caused her death. Earlier, she had described her pain by saying that there was a snake in her head. The physicians did not test for a tumor but instead categorized her as old and senile. They believed senility comes with old age and makes people talk nonsense. Their mindlessness about the category "old" blinded them to alternatives (compare Langer, 1982).

These rigid categories can be conveyed to us or may be of our own making (Chanowitz and Langer, 1981). If we approach our jobs in a particular way, day in and day out, we may lock ourselves into a distinct way of doing things and simultaneously blind ourselves to better methods as they come along. One of the fears that people may have of an educational system that creates a place for several perspectives is that nothing will remain stable; there will be nothing reliable to which we can turn for continuity. Yet we discover that, by viewing the same information through several perspectives, we become more open to it.

Consider sketches that contain two overlapping images. On first impression, one is likely to see either one or the other, but not both. At this stage, most people are quite confident that the image is clear and even after lengthy inspection are not likely to see the other image. Only after they are prompted to look at the sketch in another way are they likely to see the second image. One might introduce a third perspective by turning the sketch upside down. From this angle, the sketch might appear to be no more than a series of squiggles; however, research indicates that people usually depict figures more accurately when they copy forms from an inverted figure than they do when copying directly (Edwards, 1979).

It may be that by inverting the figure we free ourselves from preconceived categories and open ourselves to the available information. The information may remain ambiguous, but at least we have a foundation from which to work. Just as we might turn a figure upside down in order to copy it more accurately, we may view the same phenomena from several perspectives in order to discover the information buried beneath our preconceived categories. If we fail to explore several perspectives, we risk confusing the stability of our own mindset with that of the phenomena itself. And so by mindfully turning our world upside down, we help expose its underlying stability.

When we are mindless, we are stuck in a single perspective oblivious to alternatives; we may be missing a good part of the world around us—and we are missing it by default, not by design. We take raw experience, fashion it in some particular way, and then let our constructions prevent reconstructions that may better suit us. Consider a story Langer tells in her book *Mindfulness* (1989). Imagine that it is two o'clock in the morning and your doorbell rings. You answer it and see a man standing before you. He wears two diamond rings and a fur coat, and there is a Rolls Royce behind him. He is sorry to wake you at this ridiculous hour, he tells you, but he is in the middle of a scavenger hunt. His ex-wife is in the same contest, which makes it very important to him that he win. He needs a piece of wood about three feet by seven feet. Can you help him? In order to make it worthwhile, he will give you $10,000. You believe him. He is obviously rich. And so you say to yourself, how in the world can I get this piece of wood for him? You think of the lumber yard; you do not know who owns the lumber yard; in fact, you are not even sure where the lumber yard is. It would be closed at two o'clock in the morning anyway. You struggle, but you cannot come up with anything. Reluctantly, you tell him, "Gee, I'm sorry."

The next day, when passing a construction site near a friend's house, you see a piece of wood that is just about the right size, three feet by seven feet—a door. You could have just taken a door off the hinges and given it to him, for $10,000. Why on earth, you say to yourself, did it not occur to you to do that? It did not occur to you because, yesterday, your door was not a piece of wood. The seven-by-three foot piece of wood was hidden from you, stuck in the category called "door."

When categories entrap us, they may be called mindsets. In her research, Langer has called them "premature cognitive commitments" because such mindsets form before we do much reflection (Chanowitz and Langer, 1981). When we accept an impression or a piece of information without thinking critically about it (perhaps because it seems irrelevant), that impression settles unobtrusively into our minds until a similar signal from the outside world—such as sight or smell or sound—calls it up again. And the next time, it may no longer be irrelevant, but most of us do not reconsider what we thoughtlessly accepted earlier. Such mindsets, especially those formed in childhood, are obviously premature. But the mindless individual becomes committed to one predetermined use of the information, and other possible uses or applications are not explored.

## The Power of Uncertainty

Langer and Piper (1987) experimentally tested some of the effects of these premature cognitive commitments. The research they conducted illuminates the relationship between certainty and mindlessness—a relationship that may hold the key for change. Mindlessness, in fact, may help explain why we are frequently in error but rarely in doubt. Because of the similarity between the experimental treatment and the way most of us learn most of what we know (with certainty), the study they conducted also suggests how pervasive our mindlessness may be. Langer and Piper varied the way that they introduced people to objects and found that simply stating with certainty to research participants what the things were resulted in a lack of creative alternative use for them. In one group, for example, participants were told, "This is a dog's chew toy" (that was one of the many objects that were named). Another group (the experimental one) was also introduced to the same objects, but in a conditional, uncertain fashion. It was told, for example, "This could be a dog's chew toy." Based on past research, Langer and Piper expected that information presented unconditionally would not be subjected to questioning in the future, even if that turned out to be advantageous. The function of the chew toy was thus frozen, like movement in a photo. When information was accompanied by some uncertainty, the chew toy became an object to be used in many ways.

The objects in the study were presented as consumer products that were to be rated from most to least expensive. Once the subject started to write, the experimenter explained that she had made a mistake, that they were to be rated from least to most expensive. She did not have any more forms. What was she to do? The question really being asked was whether the subject would think to use the dog's chew toy as an eraser? Only those people who had been introduced to the object with some uncertainty thought of this novel use. This experiment was repeated several times and in different settings and consistently demonstrated this finding.

In the classroom, we found that learners' creativity is stifled when information is presented in an unconditional form, but that lessons taught with conditional language elicited creativity (Langer, Hatem, Joss, and Howell, 1989).

Why do we become mindless? As we will see, there is great advantage to creating categories and distinctions in the first place, as that activity is the essence of mindfulness. Creating them, however, makes possible being trapped by them. Why does mindlessness persist, in spite of its disadvantages?

Mindlessness is inadvertently taught in families and in our schools from generation to generation through the acquisition of "facts." We form premature cognitive commitments to the facts we are given without reason to question, and so they remain unquestioned. We are typically taught in school that there are, say, three reasons for the Civil War, not two or five. We are not led to consider how these historical "facts" might differ, depending on age, ethnicity, regionalism, gender, or profession. What reasons for the Civil War would be given by a twenty-five-year-old white male soldier from Alabama, and how might they differ from those of a seventy-year-old black female professional living in New York? Learners are often taught to view facts as immutable, unconditional truths.

Time and time again, we are led to look for the right answer in school. We form premature cognitive commitments to information when it is taught explicitly and probably also when information is just casually mentioned with the same certainty. Over the years, our culture has changed tremendously and might benefit from reconsideration of the basic assumptions or rules that have become part of our social fabric. Each new advance, social or technical, does not require a total revamping of our culture, our educational system, or our lives. We should, however, be open to the possibility of change when it is advantageous.

Another reason mindlessness persists is that certainty breeds mindlessness and that confidence and certainty are often confused. The more sure we are of something, the less attention we give it, be it our children, our careers, or our personal relationships. Our culture values confidence, but few of us recognize that confidence need not rest on certainty. We can be confident that we will find a solution, for example, without being certain of any single way of discovering it. Further, to the extent that we accept that the world is complex and that each aspect of it can be viewed variously, certainty about any particular way would be foolhardy. Yet it is rarely the case that we pursue alternative (perhaps better) solutions once we have found one that works. Similarly, it is unusual to search for several explanations for problems and events after we have found one that makes sense to us. We latch onto a single solution so quickly, frequently, and confidently that it comes to seem like only one.

## Multiple Perspectives

In a different vein, the culture passes on mindlessness because mindfulness is wrongly associated with stress. Ironically, stress is mindless, not mindful. Many years ago, Epictetus said that the views people take of events, not the events themselves, cause stress. If one takes a mindless or single-minded view of an event—is certain that it is going to happen and that when it does the consequences will be wholly negative—one is going to experience stress (Langer, Janis, and Wolfer, 1975). If, however, one is open to multiple views of the situation, considers how the event may be likely or unlikely, and examines the ways that the outcome may be positive, negative, or neutral, the event necessarily becomes less stressful.

Suppose that we were to stop someone in the street and say, "Excuse me. Are there multiple ways of looking at situations, or are there just single ways?" Virtually everybody is going to say that there are multiple ways. Nevertheless, we operate in the world as if there were a single understanding of events; and if these single understandings are negative, we experience the stress that most of us try to escape. Most of the time what we fear about stress is failure. Because the fear of failure keeps us mindless so much of the time, it may be useful to take a closer look at what failure is.

## The Success of Failure and the Failure of Success

A mindful look at failure reveals that, if we change the context and look at it from a different perspective, we may remove the failure. In so doing, we remove the stress and thus the reason that people are afraid to change. Too often, we as educators do not attempt to introduce a new perspective that removes failure. Instead, our attempts at educational remediation devalue the perspectives of those who are perceived to be in need of help. This devaluation may force the learner to seek compensation for a loss of self-worth. A common way of recovering from this loss is to make a favorable comparison in some other dimension—that is, to identify a way in which we are better than others, just as others have proven themselves to be better than we (Taylor, Wood, and Lichtman, 1984; Wills, 1983). Although such comparison may assist in restoring our sense of self-worth, it may also prompt us to devalue aspects of experience in order to draw these personally favorable comparisons.

Persons tend to value activities that they do well. Consequently, they devalue other activities. By valuing some and devaluing others, we ignore the many perspectives from which any activity may be viewed. At every moment in a mindful state, one is learning something; one is changing in some way; one is interacting with the environment so that both self and environment are different. From this perspective, a moment spent on one activity as opposed to another is not consequential. When one is aware that one did not accomplish a particular task because another task was completed, there is no reason to evaluate oneself negatively (Langer, 1979; Langer and Park, 1990). If all of one's time is spent achieving something, drawing distinctions, making connections, seeing and learning something, no moment is more valuable than another.

This kind of understanding should promote mindfulness. Consider this simple illustration. I drop my pen, which is clearly a clumsy thing to do. I bend down to pick it up and in doing so wrench my back. My goodness! Here are two negative events, and I end up in the hospital. It seems that to have dropped the pen and wrenched my back was clearly a personal failure for me. Now that I am in the hospital, however, for the first time and by necessity, I get a chance to review my life and to figure out what is meaningful and what is not. After all this thought, which occurred because of the time I had to reflect, I end up with a new philosophy of life. In other words, consequences have meaning within a context, and contexts keep changing. Therefore, the positive or negative aspects of the event keep changing.

Another example illustrates the same thing. A company was producing a new type of glue. Developing this innovative product was an expensive proposition, and there was a major problem. The glue failed to adhere; it was clearly a failure. Rather than abandoning the project, however, a mindful individual in the company turned the situation around and produced the post-it notes that many of us use.

While it is not surprising that failures may be mindless, it is interesting to note how success also carries with it an inclination toward mindlessness. People are trained to follow what is called a "win-stay, lose-switch" strategy. Keep doing something if it works; change it if it does not. Another expression of the same idea is "Don't fix it if it isn't broken." The problem with this approach is that there is a tendency when things work to pay no attention to them—to treat them mindlessly, that is. And then, all of a sudden, the equipment or the relationship breaks down; some big change occurs that need not have taken place if smaller problems had been dealt with earlier.

Galileo, for example, embodies the ambiguity of all human accomplishments. Sometimes viewed as one of the most intelligent persons in the history of science, Galileo relied on direct observation to transform the nature of "truth" in Western culture. Although empiricism is commonplace today, for Galileo's contemporaries it was a novelty. The vast majority of Galileo's contemporaries—following Aristotle—believed that a heavier object would fall more quickly than a lighter object until Galileo demonstrated that even unequal weight would fall at the same rate. He overturned the world view that dominated his age merely by testing it empirically.

Yet we may also see Galileo as a person trapped by his own ideas. Insisting that only what could be seen was believable, Galileo dismissed the work of his contemporary Kepler. From Galileo's perspective, Kepler's ideas—that a mysterious, unseen force (gravity) existed and that the gravitational attraction between sun and moon caused the tides—was simply unbelievable. By discounting Kepler's assertion, Galileo failed to recognize a force that we today consider self-evident. Thus, Galileo's greatest strength, his rigorous empiricism, was also his greatest limitation. If one is successful, mindlessness may prevent even greater success. It may have been Voltaire who said, "While doubt is unpleasant, certainty is ridiculous."

In essence, we have just considered the success of failure and the failure of success. Without recognizing that these categories (success/failure) go a long way toward promoting our mindlessness and preventing us from being able to change, we are apt to let our experience systematically seduce us into believing that that is the way the world works. The more successful we are, the more motivated we may be to see that it could have been no other way. The power of uncertainty is that it presses us to give up that illusion of stability and control for the power to construct our own choices. In so doing we should be able to avert the danger not yet arisen. Instead of mindlessly not noticing changes, at worst, or selecting from alternatives given to us, at best, we can be creating our own alternatives.

The way to achieve control is through mindfulness. But what does that mean? Just as mindlessness is the rigid reliance on old categories, mindfulness means the continual creation of new ones. Categorizing and recategorizing, labeling and relabeling, are processes as natural to adults as they are to children. As one masters the world, these processes are an adaptive and inevitable part of surviving. When we make new categories in a mindful way, we pay attention to the situation and the context. Being mindful, in fact, means being in the present, sensitive to context.

When we are mindful, we are more likely to respond without fear of consequences because we know that they can be multidimensional, not simply negative. Breaking out of our mindsets, we undertake more challenges because we have a fuller understanding that failure and any clear-cut idea of winners and losers no longer make sense. We can take a broader view of both ourselves and others. For instance, we are unlikely to get up in the middle of the morning and say to ourselves, "Today, I think I am going to be rigid, obnoxious, and prejudiced." Yet at least some of the time, we may be less than perfect. When we come across people who are behaving in ways that we do not accept, we often assume that it is their intention to act that way, but mindfulness research suggests that each of these negative behaviors may be interpreted in several ways. Once we select a more benign interpretation, we may come to like people we otherwise might avoid. When that other person is ourself, we may find that changing is easier than we once thought.

Many years ago, as a therapist, Langer found herself often wanting to tell clients who wanted to change, "So just change, just do it." It is inappropriate for a therapist to say such things, of course, so she silently puzzled over the fact that the things that people wanted to accomplish were well within their behavioral repertoires. They were motivated and able to change. So why not just do it? Now after over fifteen years of research, we finally understand why people do not just change.

In an informal survey, we gave people a list of adjectives and behavioral descriptions and asked them to circle all of those that represented things they had tried but were unable to change about themselves. This list consisted of terms like *impulsive, rigid, conforming, grim,* and so forth. We then took this list; changed the order in which words appeared; and unbeknownst to the research participants, substituted positive counterparts. For example, the second list contained the words *consistent* instead of *rigid, spontaneous* instead of *impulsive.* We asked people to circle on this list those words that represented qualities they valued. Essentially, we found that what people found hard to change were the same behaviors they valued most when named in a positive way.

These results suggest that, when we want to change our behavior, change may really be dependent on a decision. If we want to stop being impulsive, we may have to give up being spontaneous. When we realize that this is our choice, many of us opt not to change, and that seems sensible. Going easier on ourselves usually results in our being easier on others.

The next time somebody else is hard to change, and we find ourselves saying, "You always do. . . .", at the root may be mindlessness—our own. When other people *always* do something, it is rarely just to annoy us. They are usually doing it because it represents some behavior that they value when looked at from another perspective. Although we are often tolerant of learners' "mistakes," we are largely unwilling to view their answers, not as errors, but as responses arising from a different context. When we are mindful, we recognize that a seemingly inadequate answer works in another context. If we respect learners' capacity to define their own experience, to generate their own hypotheses, and to discover new ways of categorizing their world, we might not be so quick to evaluate the adequacy of their answers. We might, instead, begin searching for their questions.

## Conclusion

Mindfulness helps us change, then, in three broad ways. First, in a mindful mode, there is little to change because big catastrophes are kept from occurring in the first place. By being situated in the present, we notice small things as they are unfolding. Recognizing the power of uncertainty helps to keep us in the present and to observe. Deviations from habitual ways are typically no longer problematic; they become elements of an ongoing situation. Second, being mindfully aware that failure is not a rigid category, but rather depends on the situation, helps us move on to find success. Those problems that we may have inadvertently allowed to happen may be viewed as an opportunity. Finally, being mindful means being aware of multiple perspectives and being free to choose what we do and do not want to change in our education, our work, or our relationships.

CORIN: And how like you this shepherd's life, Master Touchstone?
TOUCHSTONE: Truly, shepherd, in respect of itself, it is a good life; but in

respect that it is a shepherd's life, it is naught. In respect that it is solitary, I like it very well; but in respect that it is private, it is a very vile life. Now in respect it is in the fields, it pleaseth me well; but in respect it is not in the court, it is tedious. As it is a spare life, look you, it fits my humour well; but as there is no more plenty in it, it goes much against my stomach. Hast any philosophy in thee shepherd? [Shakespeare, *As You Like It,* Act 3, scene 2].

## References

Ableson, R. P. "Beliefs Are Like Possessions." *Journal for the Theory of Social Behavior,* 1986, *16,* 223-250.

Chanowitz, B., and Langer, E. J. "Premature Cognitive Commitment." *Journal of Personality and Social Psychology,* 1981, *41,* 1051-1063.

Edwards, B. *Drawing on the Right Side of the Brain.* Los Angeles: Tarcher, 1979.

Langer, E. J. "The Illusion of Incompetence." In L. C. Perlmutter and R. A. Monty (eds.), *Choice and Perceived Control.* Hillsdale, N.J.: Erlbaum, 1979.

Langer, E. J. "Old Age: An Artifact?" In S. Kiesler and J. McGaugh (eds.), *Aging: Biology and Behavior.* San Diego, Calif.: Academic Press, 1982.

Langer, E. J. *Mindfulness.* Reading, Mass.: Addison-Wesley, 1989.

Langer, E. J., Hatem, M., Joss, J., and Howell, M. "Conditional Teaching and Mindful Learning: The Role of Uncertainty in Education." *Creativity Research Journal,* 1989, *2,* 139-150.

Langer, E. J., Janis, I., and Wolfer, J. "Reduction of Psychological Stress in Surgical Patients." *Journal of Experimental Social Psychology,* 1975, *11,* 155-165.

Langer, E. J., and Park, K. "Incompetence: A Conceptual Reconsideration." In R. J. Sternberg and J. Kolligan (eds.), *Competence Considered.* New Haven, Conn.: Yale University Press, 1990.

Langer, E. J., and Piper, A. "The Prevention of Mindlessness." *Journal of Personality and Social Psychology,* 1987, *53,* 280-288.

Taylor, S. E., Wood, J., and Lichtman, R. "It Could Be Worse: Selective Evaluation as a Response to Victimization." *Journal of Social Issues,* 1984, *39,* 19-40.

Wills, T. A. "Social Comparison in Coping and Help-Seeking." In B. M. DePaulo, A. Nadler, and J. D. Fisher (eds.), *New Directions in Helping.* Vol. 2: *Help-Seeking.* San Diego, Calif.: Academic Press, 1983.

*ELLEN J. LANGER is professor of psychology and chair of the Social Psychology Program at Harvard University. Her latest books include* Mindfulness *(Addison Wesley, 1989) and* Higher Stages of Human Development *with Charles N. Alexander (Oxford University Press, 1990).*

*JUSTIN PUGH BROWN is a graduate student in psychology at Harvard University.*

*Cultural institutions are essential agencies for stimulating and enhancing reflection and for constructing and expressing knowledge. They are places of the mind, for mindful acts.*

# Cultural Institutions as Structures for Cognitive Change

*David Carr*

Cultural institutions are valuable instruments in the lives and minds of learners because they illuminate the possibilities of thought, reflection, and inquiry. The illumination comes not only because these institutions offer pleasant experiences, convivial resources, and engaging public spaces. The illumination comes because cultural institutions are instruments for seeing and sensing the enlightening possibilities of cognitive change over the life span. These places are designed to support the unique reflections and critical processes of adulthood and to sustain the thinking that constructs continuous change in one life.

Cultural institutions surround us in many forms: they are libraries, museums, and public broadcasting stations; they are zoos, aquariums, botanic gardens; restorations, historic houses and societies, public memorials; even town squares and public parks. In all of these places, some form of information—text, artifact, living system—is named and set apart, saved and placed within the design of a logical order, surrounded and supported by connections to other informing parts of the world. And in all of these places, the cultural institution itself is made complete and complex by the presence of human beings. To see museums and libraries as cognitive instruments in the lives and minds of learners is to grasp them as places where mindful attention, active construction, and critical thinking can thrive, leading the learner toward change. As objects and information touch the lives of human beings, the possible meanings of the touch expand the horizons of thought.

Systematic observations over twenty years suggest that cultural institutions should be seen as structures for cognitive change for a number of reasons. (1) They have form and involve order; (2) that is, there is a logic to the organization. Humans are given this order by the institution and therefore do not have to invent it for themselves. (3) The setting, its contents, and the information it offers generally remain stable over time. Further, this information is typically wide in scope and flexibly presented. (4) Consequently, several levels of access are possible. (5) With increasing frequency of exposure, these levels of access and complexity are revealed to the user. Curiosity is piqued. (6) And questioning is invited. (7) Observations and participation require decision making and problem solving. (8) These decisions follow from—and make possible—the expression of desires and intentions. (9) As a result, users necessarily conceive and design their own experiences in cultural institutions. (10) They offer learners opportunities to explore and evaluate in privacy. Thinking in these settings is variable and frequently unexpressed; its pace, processes, and engagements with others vary. Whatever its form, the structure offered by a cultural institution assists the gradual evolution of cognitive change, under the control of the evolving human at its center.

In most cultural institutions, critical mental acts depend on simple but useful structures; they make possible the transmission of knowledge and the vigorous exploration of cultural experiences. Two such literal structures are embodied in familiar instruments like the card catalog and the museum map, comfortable tools that present the structural fabric of the institution to the user. They reveal an organization of the museum's contents; embedded in this are interwoven ideas and themes, arrayed over an open space. Among other such structures are book lists, thematic guides, handbooks, and orientation programs. They permit planning and suggest alternatives. Articulated systems of this kind make it possible for a learner to comprehend the institution as a territory with logic and balance, to grasp its categories and contents, and to find a fitting way through it. But the structure of any cultural institution is more than a physical array, its organization is more than categorical, and it is more than a mapmaker's territory.

Cultural institutions are organized knowledge environments, providing relatively pure access to evidence through objects, information, and experiences; they are formed and driven by knowledge and the processes of creating knowledge. They are also information systems for exploring and manipulating the evidence given; they emphasize the user's direct access to data and observations, without dependence on mediation. Cultural institutions also embody communication processes for the transmission and documentation of knowledge. They are environments where the learner's challenges are to incubate tentative thoughts, to construct coherent contexts for new information, to create boundaries for the management of cognition, and to make judgments of relevance among the available data.

Learning in cultural institutions implies several levels of information processing: the transmission and reception of data, the documentation and naming of concepts, and expansion and verification of information through further inquiry. The use of cultural institutions for learning requires active behaviors related to knowledge, information, and communication—and the redefinition of oneself as a learner, actively seeking new experiences and, through them, changes of mind.

## Cultural Institutions as Purposeful Structures, Conducive to Cognitive Change

The perspective of this chapter is based on the assumptions that cultural institutions are agencies in their cultures and that they are educative environments in adult lives, settings that offer human design and personal control over individual cognitive experiences. But more than this, their existence is a form of advocacy for the awakening of cognitive possibilities. Rather than passive repositories, cultural institutions are intentionally conducive to activities that encourage and inspire intellectual change. In museums and libraries, human beings must make decisions about the intensity and duration of their experience; they are invited to consider new and expansive information; and they are challenged to discover the innovative edges of their own skills, capacities, and strengths.

An inventory of the essential situations for learning made possible by museums and libraries includes at least the following few characteristics:

*Proximity to the evidences and sensations of objects, texts, living things.* Unlike the classroom or other system requiring an instructor, the management and design of cognition in the cultural institution remain under the control of the learner. Ultimately, the objects, texts, and living systems at hand are not mediated through the eyes or language of another human being.

*Participation through acts of inquiry and communication.* In museums and libraries, the processes of observing and defining phenomena or subjects are occasions for critical thought, often involving the perspectives and questions of others. Situations for questions occur constantly, inviting discourse and contextualization through language.

*Access to cognitions and visions of others.* Cultural institutions permit learners to experience the visionary perspectives of mentors, wizards, and geniuses, side-by-side with the more worldly perspectives of everyday companions. Models of artistry, inquiry, and connoisseurship may be present, active forces in the setting.

*The presence and influence of information.* Human attention seeks and grasps vivid information in museums and libraries, using it to construct, reflect, and remember images of the human mind, the forceful universe, the distant past.

These characteristics—the combination of evidence, inquiry, perspective, and information—compose the structures that make cognitive change possible in the museum or the library. They also cause the museum or library to be inherently challenging, even hazardous, to routine conventional thoughts. The tasks of these institutions and the situations they create are to realize this transformative power, spark insights among users, and excite alternative views of experience.

Cultural institutions illuminate possibility for the individual life. For example, the scope of the universe revealed in even a modest public library collection must extend beyond the world experienced every day. The familiar metaphors for a library are instructive: many voices are here; distant journeys are possible; it is the people's university. But each easy idea conceals a complex truth about the setting as a structure: the voices are separate, distinct, and accessible; linear connections can overcome and redefine constraining horizons; and critical authority belongs to the learner. The array of resources at hand in the forms of books, electronic files, or artifacts expands exponentially the numbers of tools or objects available for unfettered public use. And the structure that contains these resources offers relatively objective, nonrestrictive contexts for them. Learners do not have to see or use them in only one way; they can be juxtaposed in infinite combinations.

By offering intellectual control to the user over the array of available resources, the organizing structures of cultural institutions make connections, combinations, and comparisons possible. For example, the library and its primary tools use a system of subject headings to provide access to the content and location of books and other resources. Museums use form, process, chronology, social group, history, geography, and discipline to organize the presentation of information. Gardens, zoos, and aquariums display living collections according to structure, adaptation, or placement within family or environment. Not only do such structures offer the intellect certain routes of entry and access, but they also suggest logics and frames of mind through which artifacts and phenomena can be approached and related to each other.

Despite the importance of these cultural or disciplinary organizers, they are permeable boundaries; cultural institutions nourish the conduct of systematic interdisciplinary thinking. Again, easy metaphors offer some substance: cultural institutions allow journeys across disciplines; they provide infinite paths to knowledge; they permit exotic voyages. In fact, the library or museum does overcome artificial academic boundaries; it provides learners with the opportunity to construct personal paths; and the exotic voyage is always a passage of vicarious experiences from which the mind must return changed.

The structure of cultural institutions makes epistemic—knowledge-generating—work possible in ways that otherwise remain beyond experience. Great collections require critical thinking if a learner is to make the simplest decisions about attention and thought. (Where to look first? How to make choices? What way leads to the richest experience?) If the learner is to describe or connect information and objects, the exploration of vocabulary and context is necessary. (What are the evidences and contexts of luminism, the art movement concerned with the effects of light? What are the relationships among these evidences? How were they interpreted among luminists? What nearby models or authorities can be applied to the problem?) Over time, it is only among complex phenomena and accurate information that one can develop original, informed critical perspectives and master techniques for observing the subtle qualities and differences among them.

The way to understand how cultural institutions make knowledge possible is to see them as places for extraordinary encounters with other minds and new information, for exploring memories in private, for tracing connections, and, thus, for reaching beyond the immediate. Information exchanged with companions in the presence of stimulating experiences can lead us to verify or revise what we know, and the sharing of alternative perspectives can lead us to attend more closely to our own beliefs. Objective information in cultural institutions is valuable, first, because it assists us to know the immediate and to make decisions for the moment; second, we can use such information to plan future inquiries and to pursue knowledge beyond the present, perhaps in other places.

## Cultural Institutions as Working Systems for the Construction of Learning

Regardless of its specific content, every cultural institution named in the first sentences of this essay comprises multiple elements—objects, information, resources, human beings, spaces. Their juxtaposition and interaction create countless occasions for cognitive growth, ranging from simple observations to deep engagements with difficult ideas over time. Even the simplest of these cognitive acts can be seen as a challenge to the individual's everyday systems of knowledge and action. An exhibition of historic artifacts excites a new appreciation for craft. A librarian's suggestion leads the user toward the edge of a vast, previously unimagined literature. A park memorial recalls lost forebears. Spring arrives, and the botanic garden blooms, offering a steady feast of color and scent. In these ways, cultural institutions move us beyond the experiential constraints of everyday life.

Some of the cognitive challenges of cultural institutions are easily listed. First among these is our appreciation of contrast and innovation as we respond to new and unfamiliar things. Encountering something new, we are challenged to understand its authenticity against a familiar field, to integrate it with past ideas, and to find ways of describing it that mark it and make it vivid. Similarly, when we encounter a new way of seeing the familiar, the challenge is to appreciate that new angle by applying it to a range of objects within view: illumination from a different window. Encounters with the exotic, the beautiful, the original, and the unique are expansive in their own way and make new categories of meaning or value out of the familiar. Most important, perhaps, are encounters in cultural institutions that evoke those parts of ourselves we might have thought to be lost— rememberings of hope, dreams, or fears. We are at times surprised by what we remember and how powerfully its traces hold us.

As they expand the repertoire of memory, our experiences also enlarge the map of living. They add new boundaries to definitions, create greater depths of complexity, identify additional authorities whose thinking must be understood, and provide fresh perspectives that lead to differing interpretations of the world. Among the innovative and moving experiences we may encounter are those of being fascinated and becoming deeply informed. These encounters may make difficult and problematic the knowledge we have previously used to keep on course. They change our understanding of self and human values; they shake our foundations. And if we are good learners, they give us troubles we are bound to resolve.

Museums and libraries hold information and objects intended to redefine the boundaries of what we know. Like new spectacles, they challenge us constantly to resolve fuzziness in our vision, and the quality of the resolution we achieve follows from our mastery of systematic thought and inquiry. The integration of new knowledge—and the integrity of the learner—depend on good thinking in the presence of challenging information. Thus, it is important to develop vigorous concepts of *use* in museums and libraries, to envision learners as *users* of cultural institutions, and to understand learning as an *active* event in the life and the mind of the learner.

Barbara Rogoff (1990) suggests several reasons for regarding the process of learning as an event in the human system. These are also indications of the structural properties of cognitive change. In learning events, for example, active changes and the unfolding processes that they involve are the focus of attention. Events are organized and defined in relation to goals; actions have meaning in relation to specific processes. Learning strategies follow from circumstances. "Cognitive processes," Rogoff writes, "serve the function of guiding intelligent, purposeful action and interaction" (p. 29). Thinking in this way, cognition in cultural institutions should be understood as a series of critical events, sustained over time; these are probative situations involving evidence, information, and human relationships. Learning events in cultural institutions involve constant constructions of meaning through such dimensions as context, relevance, and juxtaposition and through such expressions as reflective talk.

These constructions also suggest that learning events, their goals, and their strategies are in a constant process of adjustment and redefinition. It is likely as well that the learning event in an individual life is configured by recurrent themes and generative ideas, perhaps inherited from the limits and groundings of family and school. "In this perspective," Rogoff writes, "cognitive processes are considered to be actions (e.g., remembering, thinking, perceiving) rather than objects possessed by a thinker (e.g., memories, cognitions, perceptions). . . . The thinking organism is active in participating in an event, exploring a situation, directing attention, attempting solutions. The individual is not merely a receptacle for interacting mental entities that are themselves responsible for selecting information, adding interpretations, and embellishing stimuli according to the biases of memory. Thinking is an event in which the animal seeks information relevant to functioning effectively in the environment and transforms itself to better fit its niche" (p. 31). Rogoff cites Leont'ev (who extends Vygotsky's concept) on activity as "a system with its own structure, its own internal transformations, and its own development" (Rogoff, p. 32).

In this fundamental way, the use of cultural institutions can be seen as a systematic event. The user (a human structure of knowledge and memory) approaches the cultural institution's knowledge structure, which emphasizes the meanings of genius, geography, taxonomy, chronology, or design. For the user, these forms offer productive means of understanding relationships, developments, or patterns—ways of connecting meaning to objects and ideas. This is essentially a building process; insights and logics are constructed from experience and information. It is by definition a personal process: use implies a living presence, reaching and touching, bringing an intense subjectivity to the situation of learning.

There are many forms of museum or library use connected to cognitive change. The following ones are basic in a cultural institution: planning and anticipating an experience; choosing and changing paths; observing a developmental or historical sequence; defining critical differences in evidence; naming and organizing divergent arrays of data; determining the relevance of new information; recollecting and illuminating what is remembered; revising previous knowledge; asking and answering questions of companions, of experts, and of oneself. More advanced use involves scholarly approaches to objects and texts, access to specialized resources, or particular attention from experts. Regardless of its form, the use of the museum or library for intellectual pursuits needs time, a plan, and a process; written documentation; appropriate historical perspective; access to terminology or taxonomy; and the capacity to imagine connections. Under these conditions, the mind moves forward.

## A Situation for Cognitive Apprenticeship

The adult learner in the cultural institution is not unlike a mature, but no less unfinished, version of the child learner who stands in the area described by Vygotsky (1978) as the zone of proximal development, a realm of growth that lies between unassisted and assisted performance. In the case of the adult learner, it is not the parental influence or the teacher who beckons the learner on, but the opportunity for "collaboration with more capable peers" (p. 86) in the cultural institution. These are the librarians, advisers, experts, curators, authorities, and other learners whose voices and messages shape the museum or library. These collaborative influences may offer basic information, ideas leading to innovation, and ways to experience the mutual, reciprocal, social processes that surround learning in public. Each voice, each model of mind, invites the learner to move ahead.

Seen as structures for cognitive change, cultural institutions are ideal settings for the realization of situations where cognitive apprenticeship becomes possible. As described by recent literature (for instance, Brown, Collins, and Duguid, 1989; Farnham-Diggory, 1990; Rogoff, 1990), cognitive apprenticeship is emphasized as a method adaptable to children's learning through a relationship with an experienced mentor; however, the research also suggests learning situations and structures wholly appropriate for adult growth and development in cultural institutions. Rogoff (1990) emphasizes some interactive qualities of cognitive apprenticeship that are abstracted below.

Social and intellectual skills come to the learner through situations characterized by interactivity—not isolation.

Learning is situation-specific: cognitive development follows from constructive problem solving, the use of models and tools derived from others in the situation.

Mutual engagements between the learner and the other—including the joint management of learning, the use of tools, and adaptations of the learning plan in order to move toward goals—are sources of support and nurturing growth.

This interdependent base confers a memorable shared process, eventually expanding the boundaries of the learner's thoughts and leading to internal engagements and independent constructions of the event.

The situation is an example of learning in a creative social relationship involving experience, information, and skills.

Rogoff writes about situations of cognitive apprenticeship as creative processes where individuals are sensitized to select discriminately, enabling them to "transform what is available to fit their uses." As in craft apprenticeships, these are situations where "information and skills are not transmitted but are transformed in the process of appropriation. Social activity serves not as a template for individual participation but as a stepping stone, guiding the path taken but not determining it" (1990, p. 197). More succinctly, Brown, Collins, and Duguid describe the confluence of "activity, tool, and culture" (1989, p. 40).

In this conceptualization of cognitive apprenticeship, one can hear echoes of its foundations in ideas constructed by Vygotsky: "Learning awakens a variety of internal developmental processes that are able to operate only when the [learner] is interacting with people in his environment and in cooperation with his peers. Once these processes are internalized they become part of the [learner's] independent developmental achievement" (1978, p. 90). One also hears suggestions of Michael Polanyi's idea, "indwelling"—that we comprehend things by making them interior to us, by "dwell[ing] in the parts. We may be said to live in the particulars which we comprehend, in the same sense as we live in the tools and probes which we use and in the culture in which we are brought up" ([1964], 1969, p. 148). The word *situation* evokes Eduard Lindeman: "Education is a method for giving situations a setting, for analyzing complex wholes into manageable, understandable parts, and a method which, if followed, will bring the circumstance within the area of experiment" (1926, p. 180). Dewey's concept of education by experience also resonates: "Situation and . . . interaction are inseparable from each other. An experience is always what it is because of a transaction taking place" ([1938] 1963, p. 43). Lindeman again: "We do not 'think through' problems; we act through" (1926, p. 192).

Learning and change occur best in constructive situations where transactions are characterized by (1) the transmission of trustworthy data, (2) contexts and spaces for pausing to expand and connect the information given, (3) an assisting voice who provides appropriate, expansive discourse, (4) confirmation of emerging expertise, and (5) the opportunity to recognize and savor critical or insightful moments. This last element—the moment when a critical insight is recognized—marks the emergence of an intellectually independent actor in the learning structure. We may say that this is the learner who has come to understand patterns, who attempts to "try out" the possibilities of a situation in order to discover its limits, or who discovers a need to alter the horizon.

In this way, it is possible for all museums and libraries to be (like Frank Oppenheimer's laboratory of a museum, the Exploratorium) experimental environments where learners can mark their progress and intellectual emergence in practical steps and new acts of language and thought. The museum or library, fully realized as a conceptual laboratory, provides relatively unrestricted access to tools, expert consultative assistance, and flexible systems of connection among disciplines and subjects. In the best of these settings, information is an applied art; its exchange contributes perspective as it creates continuities. To understand the use and control of information is to understand the relationship between knowledge structures and the important idea that critical cognitive growth occurs, not by accident, but through design. The task of the setting is to invite decisive moments in cognitive events, occasions for critical turning points in the design and development of the mind.

## Learning Experiences in Cultural Institutions as Comprising Various Conditions of Process

We may make some assumptions about those we know as adult learners; the first and most important is the presence in their lives of continuous unknowns: unresolved pursuits, difficult transitions, intriguing ideas, ongoing questions. Among the constant tensions of adult life, transformations and self-renewal are most daunting. It is essential to see the learner as an evolving system of knowns and unknowns, engaged in a continuous dialogue with the questions of personal experience. Paulo Freire writes, "Every entity develops (or is transformed) within itself through the interplay of its contradictions" ([1970], 1982, p. 132). Such questions may be active and current, coming out of events of the day. They may be dormant, underlying questions, in need of resolution. They may be personal; they may be professional; they may be fanciful; they must be vital. All of the true learner's questions in some way reflect unfinished experiential issues. They can be envisioned as educational remnants, unkept promises, unread books, unfinished experiments.

The adult user brings to the cultural institution an unwritten autobiography of interests, prospects, and unrealized intellectual possibilities. We might also assume that there are, among these possibilities, unarticulated systems of relationships, including complementary knowns and unknowns, incidental themes and dissonant motifs, and a host of suggestive, allied issues. We may also assume that the learner is drawn to the edge of the museum or library because of a striving toward information and experience that may address these unrealized parts of the self. Gordon Allport (1955) has described this intention to live up to images of the self as "propriate striving."

Museums and libraries exist to make collections known and useful, to assemble them in ways that human beings find accessible, and to assist cognitive striving in the presence of the unknown. Unknowns, when pursued in cultural institutions, change. They are affected by the reorganization that follows from new language and expanded definitions; by the introduction of new authorities and expert resources; and by the stimulation of access to new and relevant information structures and tools. Unknowns brought to the cultural institution by its users are also subject to alteration because they can be directly influenced by the connective competence and expansive vision of librarians, curators, and educators, whose eyes and horizons significantly differ from those of the unprepared.

These agents are prepared to offer information and to make judgments of relevance and relationship. They tend to perceive patterns in problems, and they are prepared to offer alternative paths to information. The library or the museum is the place where it is possible for the learner to expose the bare frames of personal knowledge—or ignorance—and be assisted in covering them with an informed fabric. Cultural institutions are adaptive to such constructions, because they are networks of languages, categories, and elaborations of ideas. They are ideal for the exploration of concept maps (compare Novak and Gowin, 1984) and the articulation of personal perspectives through notes and personal records. Like problem solving in other venues, the resolution of unknowns in cultural institutions benefits by consistent and thoughtful applications of the mathematician Polya's heuristic admonition to "Look at the unknown!" (1957, p. 123).

## Helping the Process of Cognitive Management in Cultural Institutions

Intellectual changes in adult lives are challenging; learners will benefit from assistance as they experience these changes. A human life requires time and reflection in order to evolve fully under the control of the learner. In museums and libraries, the conduct of change is unpredictable; it may begin from one small spark and ignite unimaginable fires. It is essential for educators to invest themselves in these unimaginable unknowns by creating appropriate conditions and situations for the right sparks to be struck and for the most flammable tinder to be touched by them. Situations conducive to great intellectual illumination can be designed by educators in cultural institutions.

Several guides toward helping adults to change in cultural institutions follow. In considering them, it may be useful to suggest three metaphors to frame the cultural institution as a critical agency for intellectual growth. First, the cultural institution is a *workshop,* where certain tools—in the forms of objects, information, and processes—are used to construct relationships and patterns. Second, the cultural institution is a *conservatory* for the cultivation of acumen and skilled performances under expert mentors. Third, the cultural institution is a *greenhouse,* where the mind can be separated from distracting or threatening outer elements; situations are intentionally created to nurture awareness. Whether the professional helper takes the form of craftsperson, mentor, or horticulturist, the following suggestions will help to build a structure that invites, assists, and sustains cognitive change among adult learners.

**Create a Situation Where Learners Grasp Tools and Invent Processes.** Learning has to happen with tools literally in hand. In any situation where people are expected to learn independently, for example, the presence of extensive information resources, appropriate instruments, alternative media, and information technologies must exist. These resources often carry entire cognitive systems with them. Barbara Rogoff defines some of the "inherited" cultural tools that support problem solving to include "Language systems that organize categories of reality and structure ways of approaching situations, literate practices to record information and transform it through written exercises, mathematical systems that handle numerical and spatial problems, and mnemonic devices to preserve information in memory over time" (1990, p. 51). Further, the discovery of ways to explore, plan, and set priorities for learning cannot occur without the presence of a horizon and compass-like indications of direction; every voyager needs the polestar.

**Help Learners to Learn from Other Learners.** Dialogue hastens the emergence of the learner. A setting dedicated to fostering intellectual change will strive to create situations where learners have direct experiences with others, especially those whose questions are articulate and whose attention to learning is fresh. To whatever extent a situation for learning provides access to other minds—the minds of mentors, models, consultants—the likelihood of mutual exchange and assistance is greatly increased. The importance of the learner's access to this richness cannot be overemphasized: it helps the learner to approach evidence reflectively; it is conducive to mutual affirmation and discourse; and it assists prosocial participation and contribution. These verifications of process and commonality can reduce the isolation of the individual learner. The creation of a community of inquirers—something any cultural institution can do—will also advance comparative, critical thinking, as well as public awareness of learning.

**Emphasize the Learner's Experience as an Original Path.** Help learners to be discoverers, to think of their learning as innovation. By enabling the learner to encounter an original object or idea as discovered evidence—valuable, unmediated data directly available to the senses—the cultural institution infuses itself with power. Among all information processed in an art museum, for example, none is more essential or formative than the private moments between the user and the object. Its parallel in any library is the lingering turn of a page, the discovery of a resonant passage. These moments are irreplaceable, and their aftermath is unpredictable. Only on this foundation can authentic situations for interpreting and responding to experience be grounded.

**Undergird Practice with Theories and Values.** Situations for learning improve wherever attention is paid to the methodologies, logics, and processes. A strong institution works to articulate its principles of design, its care for learners, and its assumptions about how the institution is to be used as an instrument for learning. This kind of self-examination is never easy, but it is a critical process based on the idea that the institution is a system of knowledge embodying professional integrity and public trust: What knowledge is it possible to attain here? What does the institution demand of its learners? What does it give in return? How might the processes of learning and change best be assisted? Answers to these difficult questions are essential if styles of helping are to fit styles of learning and are to foster the gradual evolution of the learner. This exploration is best done in public; that is, *with* the public. Learning is not a process of secrets. It is important to help learners to review their progress and to understand the logic of the processes they undergo.

**Cultivate and Employ a Reflective Stance.** The most valuable agents of change will think and communicate with each other and the public about the processes of giving help to learners; they will invite collaboration in the design of programs and systems. In this way, it is possible not only to create a responsive institution, but also to explore the processes and behaviors of helping in a reflective way. There are moments in adult inquiry that demand a pause for analysis: the immediate experience should be seen as one part of the human system's evolution. Helpers, for example, should attend to and assist the evolution of a learner's focus; they should explore errors and ambiguities of vision. The reflective practitioner will consider problems to be opportunities for insight and every action to be an experiment (Schön, 1983). When certain major themes are apparent in an inquiry, it is useful to articulate and emphasize them. Focus groups and semistructured interviews can explore the quality of the institution's stance toward the learner. Novak and Gowin (1984) suggest techniques for concept mapping, a productive process for evoking and giving form to tacit ideas. It is also generally useful to cultivate emerging, still-open questions in any situation for learning, so that the learner understands the possibility that inquiries can continue into the future. Moreover, it is helpful to demonstrate that there is a heuristic value in using words to give shape to unknowns.

**Think of Every User as a Problem Solver in Need of a Process.** In a large sense, the learner's problem is the continuous need to become more finished, more fully engaged in the completion of a personal reality (Freire, 1982). The value of a heuristic approach that assists general problem-solving processes can be made clear to learners in any cultural institution. This means (1) assisting people to think of their purposes and hopes, (2) to clarify the unknown that invites them, (3) to give words to the change they wish to create, and (4) to document the evolution of an inquiry as it is constructed. The tasks of serious learners require thinking about limits, defining essential vocabularies, articulating tentative statements of goals, understanding the press of time constraints, and identifying available resources beyond the institution. An appropriate plan or schedule will help to make change possible over time. The added benefit of an articulated heuristic plan is that it confers on the user the identity of problem solver.

**Undermine Anonymity, Impersonality, Distance.** Identity is critical to inquiry: the process of learning is the way toward a self-designed life. It may sound lofty, but it is useful to help learners to see themselves as striving to realize their individual destinies in the library or the museum. Of course, this ambition is lofty; it should be. Lives brought to the cultural institution have been forged genetically, educationally, professionally, personally—and accidentally. Everyone has an individual history as a learner and an individual chance at inquiry. In order to instill ownership of the inquiry and its processes, this individual story is worth telling, and the questions that are inspired by that life are worth asking. Such self-presentation, too, is a form of inventory that assists the learner and the educator to see who is present and what their lives confer on the institution. It is a way to defeat routines and avoid the hardening of communication that can accompany institutional life.

**Help Learners to Move Beyond the Situation.** Any cultural setting is only one limited resource; its intellectual experiences must have limits as well. Learners need to move beyond its boundaries in order to develop critical insights from a comparative perspective and to understand how distance affects vision. Learners also need to derive support and verification as learners from other settings. Among the critical behaviors needed by every learner are generic pursuit skills: ways to conduct future independent learning anywhere.

**Everybody Write.** Learners and helpers should write for three reasons. First, write to keep track of learning steps, changes in process, and the complexity of ideas flowing through experience. Second, write to use personal language for abstract concepts and to create an autobiographical reference document for the illumination of the learning life. Third, write to represent the cognitive experiences of that life as lived passages in the complex system that is one organism. That is, write to synthesize what one comes to know, what one understands and feels about this knowledge, and the processes and experiences of knowing.

**Assess All Possibilities.** Finally, as an inquiry concludes, it is time to address the progress and the future of learning and the learner. What are the next steps for a learning life? Where could it best go next?

## Learning in Cultural Institutions as a Mutually Critical Event for the Agent and the Learner

Cultural institutions are human systems, embodiments and transmitters of sustaining knowledge. They are, in the words of Freire (1982), "present, existential, concrete situation[s], reflecting the aspirations of the people" (p. 85)—where aspirations may be read as power over intellectual tools and full possession of an identifiable cultural history. As structures for the transmission of information and communication among different minds, cultural institutions are subject to the design of caring, helping professionals—librarians, curators, and educators—to make the processes of learning more inviting and engaging. But these structures are also responsive to informed, planned use by critical adult learners. The mediations of professionals can redefine cultural institutions as situations and structures for learning—places where questions emerge, where dialogues occur, and where public learners can change their minds. Similarly, highly developed patterns of public use can fulfill these situations, can demonstrate their importance to a civilization, and can make them powerful. A strong cultural institution is a system that advocates independent learning through innovative perceptions, critical thinking in the face of ambiguity, and attention to detail in the presence of original ideas. These are the adult behaviors that thrive at the edges of experience.

## References

Allport, G. *Becoming*. New Haven, Conn.: Yale University Press, 1955.
Brown, J. S., Collins, A., and Duguid, P. "Situated Cognition and the Culture of Learning." *Educational Researcher*, 1989, *18* (1), 32–42.
Dewey, J. *Experience and Education*. New York: Collier, 1963. (Originally published 1938.)
Farnham-Diggory, S. *Schooling*. Cambridge, Mass.: Harvard University Press, 1990.
Freire, P. *Pedagogy of the Oppressed*. New York: Continuum, 1982. (Originally published 1970.)
Lindeman, E. *The Meaning of Adult Education*. New York: New Republic, 1926.
Novak, J. D., and Gowin, D. B. *Learning How to Learn*. New York: Cambridge University Press, 1984.
Polanyi, M. *Knowing and Being*. Chicago: University of Chicago Press, 1969. (Originally published 1964.)
Polya, G. *How to Solve It: A New Aspect of Mathematical Method*. (2nd ed.) Princeton, N.J.: Princeton University Press, 1957.
Rogoff, B. *Apprenticeship in Thinking: Cognitive Development in Social Context*. New York: Oxford University Press, 1990.
Schön, D. *The Reflective Practitioner: How Professionals Think in Action*. New York: Basic Books, 1983.
Vygotsky, L. S. *Mind in Society: The Development of Higher Psychological Processes*. Cambridge, Mass.: Harvard University Press, 1978.

*DAVID CARR is associate professor of library and information studies at the School of Communication, Information, and Library Studies, Rutgers University.*

*Action learning often challenges existing rules, experiments with truth, questions the efficacy of mediating institutions, and leads to significant personal and social change.*

# Social Advocates and Action Learning: The Discontent Dancing with Hope

*Robert L. Williams*

For most of us, the learning we associate with change in our lives follows as the *consequences of a transition*. Promoted to a new position, we acquire the necessary skills and knowledge. Grief-stricken by the death of a spouse, we adapt to loneliness and learn to do things the deceased partner used to do. Social expectations, rituals, and cultural norms aid this learning process by establishing what should be learned, the manner in which it should be learned, and the kinds of learning that will be accepted and rewarded. Transitions commonly follow patterns or take place because of expectations related to our age (midlife crisis), our age cohorts (Baby Boomers), historical or natural disasters (victims of the Great Depression or hurricanes), social desirability (law-abiding citizens), or cultural norms (traditions of white, Anglo-Saxon males) (Datan, 1983; Reese and Smyer, 1983).

In other words, we learn to *adapt* to a new role based upon predetermined expectations of it. What we learn, even if we are self-directed in that learning, follows from a set of assumptions or beliefs about society and how we fit into it. In this view of learning and personal development, the society stays the same, and the person adapts by learning about expectations and the skills and information needed to fulfill them (Lieberman, 1975; Brubaker, 1986). Learning follows as a consequence of a transition.

Not all learning follows as an adaptation to, or consequence of, transition. A much less common, but powerful and socially significant style of learning creates a *transition of consequence*. Rather than accept a particular social role, cultural attitude, or popular perspective and begin learning the necessary skills, attitudes, knowledge, and adaptive behaviors most often associated with them, some individuals resist adaptation and begin a learning process that questions the validity of the transition and the new role.

Previously viewed as deviant or nonnormative behavior, I would propose that this second learning style, described by some as "action learning" (Brandstadter, 1984 and 1985), is an important and necessary attribute of social and organizational change. Why? Unlike most forms of learning, action learning questions the basic tenets and assumptions through a nonnormative life event that is "not only expressive of the individual behavioral plasticity that characterizes our species but may also be the forerunner of social change, and thus of adaptive radiation—the biologist's term for diversification that maximizes a species's chances for survival in a changing environment" (Datan, 1983, p. 40).

In her study of individuals caring for a dependent spouse, Brubaker (1986) suggested that most of the developmental tasks involved in aging represent adaptation to changing bodily ability. In one rather poignant piece of data, she reported on the nonadaptive behavior of a man whose wife was institutionalized. He did not want to change their life patterns and was constantly confronting institutional staff over regulations and procedures. Brubaker implied that this form of nonadaptive behavior was bad in that it represented a futile battle against social norms for aging and institutionalization.

Her assumption that compliant behavior was in the best interest of the elderly person does not hold true in other studies, however. In a study of another group of elderly who had to change residences, Lieberman (1975) found that the ones who coped best "were aggressive, irritating, narcissistic, and demanding . . . [and] certainly were not the most likeable elderly" (p. 155). Those who changed residences without noticeable effects on physical or mental health had a "certain amount of magical thinking and perceiving oneself as the center of the universe, with a pugnacious stance toward the world—even a highly suspicious one—[and] seemed more likely to insure homeostasis in the face of a severe crisis" (pp. 155-156).

The juxtaposition of these two studies is startling. Brubaker argued that *accepting* the situation signals a successful adaptation whereas Lieberman argued that *preserving* an internal positive view of personhood, even if it means resisting the situation, signals a successful adaptation. In one, adaptation means totally accepting the new environment; in the second, adaptation means changing the environment. Who is right?

To further explore this notion of action learning as a component of both personal and social change, I interviewed thirteen American social advocates over three years about their transition from relatively apolitical lives to those of social advocacy. They seemed to be individuals who had tested the rules and taken new models for social justice, political participation, and economic behavior into action. For the purposes of the study, I defined *social advocates* as individuals who (1) represented a minority view; (2) took personal risks to express that view; (3) used direct action, including civil disobedience and resistance, to effect social change; (4) were part of small group that first brought a social issue to public attention; and (5) have been recognized by the media, other institutions, and affected people as an advocate (Williams, 1989).

The group of American social advocates interviewed consisted of the following: Cesar Chavez, who called the first grape boycott to improve working conditions for migrant Hispanic farmworkers around Delano, California, in 1965; Gail Sams, "an ignorant mountain woman" from Bumpass Cove, Tennessee, who spoke up in 1979 about chemicals washing into the clear creek beside her home; Helen Caldicott, a Boston physician, who called attention to the hazards of nuclear weapons testing in 1971; Albert Turner, Sr., a farmer from Marion, Alabama, who demanded voting rights for black Americans in the rural South in 1962; the late Mitch Snyder; Harold Moss, Carol Fennelly, and Ed Guinan, members or former members of the Community for Creative Non-Violence in Washington, D.C., who fasted for the poor and homeless in 1978; Kimi Gray, a welfare mother living in the Kennilworth section of Washington, D.C., who in 1966 made her initial efforts to improve the conditions of public housing; John Snyder, a Congressional aide in Washington, D.C., who first spoke in 1974 about the loss of a "basic freedom"—the right to keep and bear arms; Ellen Haas, a Silver Spring, Maryland, mother and housewife, who led the first of the consumer boycotts in 1971; Mary Sinclair, a technical writer at "the Dow" in Midland, Michigan, who began opposition to the construction of a nuclear power plant in 1967; and Candy Lightner, a realtor in Dallas, Texas, who in 1980 spoke out against drunk driving.

## Defining Action Learning

*Action learning* can be defined as the process of combining an abstract mental construct (usually moral, philosophical, or political reasoning) with a physical action that often lies outside social, economic, and political norms of behavior, both to test the validity of the construct and to reconstitute the social rules related to it (Brandstadter, 1984 and 1985; Williams, 1989). In all the cases I have examined, action learning involved some challenge to common perceptions or current paradigms of thinking.

Action learning differs from active learning in that action learning implies that the learner develops new behaviors, competencies, attitudes, or knowledge at the same time that the learner attempts to change the social context. The learner uses personal action to redefine the social context and to learn how to function in that new context. "Active learning," on the other hand, describes a common learning style that depends on learners doing more than just reading or listening to new information.

Cesar Chavez saw similarities between the above definition of action learning and what "Ghandi meant by 'experimenting with truth' " (personal communication, May 31, 1988). Action, for the advocates, becomes a way of putting into practice and externalizing new moral meaning. In so doing, the advocates I interviewed explained that they are doing more than demonstrating new behavior or attitudes for others, but that they are "acting out" concepts that remain poorly formed in thoughts and inadequately described in words. Therefore, action in this context presupposes "that action is not simply behavior, but rather self-planned behavior that can be interpreted as a means to achieve certain goals, to express certain values, or to solve certain problems, and that is—within certain boundaries— freely (or at least subjectively freely) chosen on the basis of certain beliefs and values" (Brandstadter, 1984, p. 10).

Action learning also appears to demand a certain tolerance for ambiguity and lacks specific steps to sharply defined goals. Others (Bandura, 1977; Brandstadter, 1984 and 1985; Lerner and Busch-Rossnagel, 1981; and Nesselroade and Von Eye, 1985) have implied that taking action as a way of shaping one's own development is always a clearly and premeditatively constitutive act. Nevertheless, the advocates describe the process differently. For them, taking action may be the way to clarify the next step in the transition, a means of testing options, or a way in which to explore the validity of an attitude or perception. Based upon those descriptions, I suggest that action learning may often be based on intuition, or as Helen Caldicott expressed it, on "following your nose" (personal communication, September 15, 1986).

Action learning is not the same as practicing a new skill (such as hitting golf balls off a practice tee), demonstrating known concepts (such as breeding fruit flies to demonstrate the laws of genetics), or experiential learning (such as a medical internship or practice teaching). All of these activities clearly inhabit the field of adult learning and personal development. However, they tend to be ways of learning the basic rules, rather than experimenting with them (Bandura, 1977; Brandstadter, 1984; Lerner and Busch-Rossnagel, 1981; and Nesselroade and Von Eye, 1985). Obviously, few learning experiences display only one style of learning.

## Steps in Action Learning

Out of the interviews with the social advocates, I identified three steps of action learning: testing the old rules, acting out new concepts, and learning from action.

**Testing the Old Rules.** For the social advocates, the first step in action learning was to test the old rules by asking difficult questions of themselves. Which of my beliefs do I understand and practice? What do I fear and why? Do I follow the rule because it is easier or because it is right? For Harold Moss, an early member of the Community for Creative Non-Violence, the dialogue focused on obedience: "I'm accustomed to being obedient, I'm accustomed to, if somebody asks me to do something for them, to do it for them. Why should I resist? Why should I go against a policeman who asked me to move? That was a very profound thing for me, along with a lot of other things. I had to learn that to resist was a prophetic and necessary thing to do" (Harold Moss, personal communication, April 11, 1988).

Albert Turner, Sr., remembered clearly the element of fear when he walked up the steps of the columned Perry County Courthouse for the first time to register to vote. He took the voter registration test and failed. (The tests were often different for blacks and whites. Blacks would be asked to quote, from memory, an obscure amendment from the Constitution and explain its meaning.) He took it again and failed. He went back again and again and again, failing every time. Each visit to the courthouse was a way to test the rules and to focus on the problem. "At first, I didn't believe I would fail the test. I was a college graduate. I knew they would let me register. If I ever began to doubt what I was doing, I just went down and tried to register" (Albert Turner, Sr., personal communication, May 25, 1988).

Mitch Snyder viewed the first step in action learning as breaking the cyclic dilemma of finding moral *reasons* to justify action, rather than taking action in response to moral *reasoning*. The first sequence he called "truth," the second he called "meaning":

> At some point you have to say things to people that they may not want to hear because that's an act of service no less than serving a bowl of soup. We all hunger for many things: the material are only the easiest to deal with, most readily available and the easiest to satisfy. We also hunger for meaning rather than "answers" or "the truth." We also rebel against hearing [meaning] because it makes demands on our lives if our lives aren't rooted totally in truth and decency and service and resistance and all the rest. But the ability to affect people or to cause them to respond is probably in direct correlation to the consistency with which one lives one's life. The longer you've been doing this and the more people are aware of what you're doing, the more power is attached to your words" [Mitch Snyder, personal communication, April 10, 1988].

**Acting Out New Concepts.** The second step in action learning is to act out the emerging mental construct in both its positive and negative aspects. In the early 1960s, Fishman and Solomon (1963) interviewed one of the four black freshmen at North Carolina A & T who began the student sit-ins by simply occupying stools at a segregated lunch counter in downtown Greensboro, North Carolina, on February 1, 1960. They were motivated by a combination of action for social change and action for personal change. Fishman and Solomon called the second reason "pro-social acting out." By taking a passive and pious stance, they said, the black students provoked white extremists to "act out for them the very anger and resentment that they [the blacks] have themselves felt" (p. 879). The advocates I interviewed also described the concept of acting out inexpressible experiences and emotions, but they also talked about the need to act out inexpressible values emerging from concepts of economics, politics, social justice, or fair housing. Acting out was a time to experiment with the truth and to create more dimensions for their new role.

Lachman, Lachman, and Butterfield (1979) described the psychological process for the creation of new paradigms (or new perceptual sets) that are shaped by the positive aspects of old paradigms: "Some influences [of the antecedents] are positive, and certain aspects of old paradigms are retained by new paradigms. Other influences are negative; the new approach takes a form that is expressly different from its predecessor. . . . Hence, the deficiencies of one paradigm may shape the [strengths] of its successor" (p. 35).

Money, for Cesar Chavez, presented an early obstacle to his ability to become an advocate. But after he had been unemployed for several months, Chavez knew his action had removed an obstacle to his development: "After we began to not be so concerned with ourselves: how we looked, what we ate, and what we said, we began to find out a lot of beautiful things. We began to find out how people really were. We began to find out that the poorer they are, the more open they are, and the more beautiful they are. I'm not saying poverty is beautiful. I'm saying poverty is beautiful when you can make a choice" (Cesar Chavez, personal communication, May 31, 1988).

Not only would Chavez's action in walking away from a paycheck influence his own process for finding a public voice, but it would also serve as a model for other Hispanics: "We began to get other people, farm workers, who began to say, 'All right we'll give up our income.' It wasn't long before the strike started. So when the strike started, those of us in the movement had already shown we could live without paychecks. In fact, it was a little better because we didn't have any financial help before. After the strike, we began to get financial help. So it became, in a way, easier because a group of us had been doing it before" (Cesar Chavez, personal interview, May 31, 1988).

**Learning from Action.** In the third step, the social advocates found that, by taking action related to a new mental concept, they increased the flow of information about it. What had begun as a testing of old rules or assumptions, and had led to an indistinct new concept acted out in public, was now filling with specifics, examples, necessary steps, and clear objectives. By taking action, the advocates invited reaction, which involved others in learning more about the concept.

Mary Sinclair found in her transition that, even with her passion for information, certain actions did not "happen the way you think," said Sinclair. "But if you involve yourself, there are things that start happening. You link up with other people, and things happen" (Mary Sinclair, personal communication, October 1, 1987).

Early in her emerging advocacy, one of the tenants challenged Kimi Gray's concept of empowering tenants of public housing to manage their own buildings and their own lives. The woman told Gray that they could never manage the units: "How could we manage it? I said, 'Can we do any worse than them?' I mean, everything we do has got to be successful. We are labeled the worst property in the city, got the highest crime, the highest drop-out rate, the most welfare recipients, the most everything. I mean, what can we do wrong? It's already happening wrong every day" (Kimi Gray, personal communication, May 18, 1988).

## A Model for Action Learning

From my interviews with social advocates, I learned that the reconstitution of basic social and intellectual rules or assumptions inherent in action learning invites a challenge. The advocates described four types of challenges that shaped (both positively and negatively) their development and their learning of new ways to view old problems and social issues: challenges from within, challenges from mediating institutions, challenges in implementing action learning, and challenges from their own experiences.

**Challenges from Within.** Their own self-doubts and cultural conditioning limited their ability to learn and guide their own development. Albert Turner, Sr., tells of the need to move early voter registration meetings to houses and places of business that had no connection with whites. "We constantly had to stop thinking like a 'white folks' man. In starting this kind of thing, you had to always try to find somebody who was not employed by the white people or could be pressured easily by them" (Albert Turner, Sr., personal communication, May 25, 1988).

Action learning follows a narrow line of tension or path of "equilibration" (Piaget, 1954) between our desire for self-preservation and our desire for self-transformation (Kegan, 1982, p. 45).

The process required the advocate to face certain facts or "reluctantly swallowed truths" (Harold Moss, personal communication, April 11, 1988). Gail Sams contrasted her interest in "bad news" before and after her move to public advocacy: "It's more comfortable to be innocent, because you don't have to be involved. At one time, I was one of those people: if something bad was happening, I wanted to turn it off" (Gail Sams, personal communication, May 22, 1988).

The learning process for most of the advocates reflected a similar unsettling or reconfiguration of the way they thought about and viewed the world. The construction of new perceptual sets seemed to grow, with some difficulty, out of new "expectancies" (Combs, Richards, and Richards, 1976, p. 104), new "direct or vicarious opportunities" (Combs, Richards, and Richards, 1976, p. 96), and even out of new dreams or imagination (Park, 1973).

The advocates also pointed to the conceptual challenges of a "crucial event" (Frank and Schonfield, 1967, p. 115) that began the transition to social advocacy and was marked by strong emotions such as fear, anger, depression, shock, surprise, exhilaration, and others. Candy Lightner had a son severely injured by one drunk driver and a daughter killed several years later by a second one. Albert Turner, Sr., was beaten and threatened with death for his constant attempts to register to vote.

**Challenges from Mediating Institutions.** Even organizations and institutions that supported the relevant issues were often slow in making room for the advocates' action. Chavez eventually left Saul Alinsky's Community Services Organization because it would not sanction Chavez's desire to use more direct means of addressing the needs of Hispanics. Ellen Haas tried working for a legislative committee on consumer issues, and John Snyder worked for the National Rifle Association, but both found that those organizations were not receptive to the notion of action learning.

Chavez explained that the process of testing the rules also involved the process of losing faith. Raised devoutly Catholic, Chavez found churches that would not even admit Hispanics for services. Mary Sinclair was asked to leave her small town church when her action learning challenged local civic and community leaders.

Gail Sams knew that local health departments had been out many times to take samples of water in Bumpass Cove Creek, but she had no idea what happened to the reports. She eventually learned that a Tennessee "sunshine" law made all of that information available to the public.

**Challenges in Implementing Action Learning.** Most of us have to view life as a choice between two alternatives: making history or making life (Flacks, 1976). Flacks suggested that except for the very rich and the very powerful, "We are compelled toward everyday living because it is real, it is required and it is right" (p. 264). Others who have studied the long-term effects of early political socialization on former student activists also found that, when those activists began assuming family obligations and taking jobs, their participation decreased (see, for example, Fendrich and Krauss, 1978; Maidenberg and Meyer, 1970). Residents close to the Three-Mile Island nuclear disaster who were affected but chose not to participate in activist behavior claimed that they were preoccupied with family (Walsh and Warland, 1983, p. 773).

Mary Sinclair remembered returning from one of the first conferences she attended on nuclear power and feeling overwhelmed by the task of learning she had set for herself: "I started then about what had to be done, and it really shook me up. I had all this stuff set out on the table, and it was a very real experience. But then I just decided I had no choice. To live with myself I had to just put one foot in front of the other and see where it went" (Mary Sinclair, personal communication, October 1, 1987).

**Challenges from Their Own Experiences.** Once the advocates put their self-direction into action, they found themselves challenged by the experience itself. They had many different ways of expressing what happened to their own images of advocacy and social change once they began to experience their own transitions. For some, it was moving straight toward the challenge, even if, like Albert Turner, Sr., and Gail Sams, they had initially sought to avoid public voice. For others, taking the first action learning steps gave them access to people, organizations, and ideas that pushed them beyond their initial concept of advocacy. Mitch Snyder spoke for many of them when he explained what action learning meant for him: "We tend to take it one step at a time, and we tend to have clarity one step at a time. Whether it was opening our home as a shelter, which ultimately led to all kinds of other things. Or deciding it was time for a federal building to be used as a shelter, deciding it was time to stop closing it down at the end of winters and finally getting somebody to put money into a place to make it a decent place for people to live. All of that unfolds one step at a time for us."

## Dancing with the Discontent

A limited number of interviews, as rich as they are in qualitative insight into a significant life transition, do not provide adequate grounds to generalize upon the importance of action learning within populations experiencing other forms of human development. The data does suggest some interesting questions for further discussion and exploration.

**The Learning Power of Marginality.** Social psychologists and political scientists have grappled for years with fundamental questions of empowerment and control among disadvantaged populations. The evidence has typically been bleak (for instance, Berger and Neuhaus, 1977; Cook, 1983; Freire, 1968; Gore and Rotter, 1963; Karp, 1986; Ledrer, 1986; McPhail, 1971; Mitchell, 1984; Piven and Cloward, 1977; Runciman, 1966; Shingles, 1981; Vanneman and Pettigrew, 1971). For the most part, political and social activism has been viewed as arising from feelings of deprivation (either real, relative, or perceived), tempered by degrees of feelings of control.

My interviews with social advocates suggest something else: there is a significant learning power inherent, not in deprivation, but in marginality. Whereas deprivation appears to be a negative influence on development, empowerment, and social activism, marginality seems to be liberating. Most of the advocates came from families that were marginal in some way to the central dominant culture, but not isolated. The father of Albert Turner, Sr., was one of the few land-owning blacks in Alabama. He could vote. His money was sought by area merchants. Cesar Chavez came from an early Spanish land-grant family in New Mexico. Only after losing their land in the Depression did they become migrant farm workers.

Traditions of marginality allowed the advocates to experience two different cultures: the potential of the affluent dominant society and the discrimination of the minority society. They talked of their ability to move fairly easily between the two cultures. They were able to operate successfully away from the culture of origin and to display a multicultural perspective in describing social issues. It is this tradition of marginality that distinguishes the advocates from many of their ethnic, socioeconomic, and cultural peers. They had experienced or witnessed possibilities of other cultures, becoming in the process "the discontent dancing with hope" (Geschwender and Geschwender, 1973, p. 409).

A tradition of marginality also contributed to the advocates' ability to test established rules. They displayed an ability to question and pose alternative visions that drew upon their experiences with both cultures. They also appeared less embedded in any one cultural framework. In some way, action learning links with a tradition of marginality to produce significant new visions of social and personal change. We need to know more about why that happens.

**Letting Loose of Learning.** Among all of the advocates' descriptions of organizational challenges to their transition into social advocacy, the one most damning was their almost universal suspicion of formal educational organizations. They presented examples of personal educational experiences that sought to undermine and belittle minority cultures, of educational institutions that used a "socialization placebo" to reduce the chance of real social change, and of adult learning that claimed to teach leadership, empowerment, and civic skills but that retreated when students sought to put the principles into practice.

Mary Sinclair and Gail Sams both described how they had been misled for years that the abundance of technical information on nuclear power plants and toxic waste was being critically examined at some level. Instead, they found numbers of research reports carefully filed but never used in policy decisions. Cesar Chavez, Mitch Snyder, and Kimi Gray all spoke of education programs designed to empower minority or poor adults that were led by individuals unable to give up sufficient control to allow the students to experience power. For them, formal educational institutions suppress any attempts by students for action learning.

Are our educational institutions and formal adult learning programs designed to divert discontent away from real social change? We need to know more about how power and control of the learning process present a barrier to action learning.

**Action Learning in Other Contexts.** Even though most of my discussion has focused on the action learning experiences of social advocates, I believe the implications for other forms of personal development are obvious. Patterned transitions, even when highly successful and financially rewarded, may actually stifle personal development. I found myself using many of the experiences of social advocates to analyze my own development. At what points in my life did I ask significant questions about the assumptions that guided and supported me? In retrospect, there were times when I should have questioned the moral assumptions underlying decisions, but at many other times I should have questioned the "rules" that were only figments of organizational mythology.

The spirit of testing established rules seems equally important to many other social roles. In fact, it suggests some element of moral reasoning as a key component of any transition or even any learning experience. Increasingly in medicine and science, the important questions are no longer technical, but rather moral and social. The same can be said for banking and teaching. Perhaps a more action-oriented learning process would enhance both personal and professional development in a broad number of settings.

**Implications for Adult Education.** Of the many hundreds of thousands of courses and programs educators offer adult learners, few, if any, address specifically the process of change for individuals and societies. We bemoan the fact that primary and secondary education does little to prepare students for lifelong learning. Perhaps we are too hasty in blaming others for overlooking one-half of the universal equation for self-development when we ourselves have underemphasized the other half.

Action learning becomes a central process for learning about change and one of the few adult education philosophies to emphasize the cognitive and philosophical reordering that fuels and follows learning. (Jack Mezirow's writing on taking perspectives (1985; Collard and Law, 1989) certainly provides more support and specifics on the adult learner in profound learning experiences that reorder moral and intellectual realities.)

There are at least three ways adult educators can encourage action learning. First, they can assist learners in "peeling the onion" of theory and practice that have produced the current acceptable rules in any area. To do so, the adult educator should focus upon the divergent, rather than convergent, paths of theory development. What was known and discarded? What is proposed, but not popular? What diverges from current thinking and why? What works or does not work in the learner's setting, even if it does not fit the "norm." (The theory and practice of quality circles, total quality management, and self-managed teams reflect principles of action learning.)

Second, adult educators can help adults explore the moral dimensions of their development and learning (see, for example, Fowler, 1981; Gilligan, 1982). Specifically, adult educators should ask adult learners to explore *all* the consequences of their learning, not just the benefits of education. For instance, I participated in educational programs in the rural South in the late 1960s and early 1970s that helped young rural blacks find admissions and resources to postsecondary education. Unfortunately, we never helped them deal with the lack of jobs in their home towns; as a consequence of their learning, they were forced from their communities. We thus deprived sections of the rural South of a significant human resource. Principles of action learning would suggest that the "economic rules" of the rural South should have been simultaneously reconstituted to make more room for well-educated blacks.

Third, adult educators need to realize that in action learning even the teacher, the methods, and the educational institution will come under scrutiny. Because ontogeny recapitulates phylogeny even within social organizations, educational institutions frequently play a significant role in passing along social norms. Learning that challenges those norms or rules often challenges the teachers themselves, who react by limiting the students or the curriculum.

In the chocolate-growing regions of the state of Cera along the coast of Brazil, I saw a school on a large estate. The owners lived in Rio de Janeiro, and the land was worked and the cocoa bean harvested by peasants using only human and mule power. Daily, the peasant children living on the estate attended both primary and secondary school, supposedly to receive a technical education suitable for home economics, agriculture, and civil engineering.

By all evidence and measures, the students were learning the skills to support economic growth. They also engaged in action learning, partly because much of what they learned underscored the inequalities around them and partly because the school was run with principles of self-governance, democratic decision making, social justice, and moral theory to run the school—everything from rules of behavior and discipline, to dormitory assignments, to curriculum. I think one or two generations of this type of action learning will lead to more change than the landowner intended.

Action learning creates previously unanticipated change. In an interactive process among student, teacher, community, and the body of knowledge, the roles and the rules begin to blur and merge in unpredictable ways. What evidence of the butterfly can be found in the worm? Where do the discontented learn to dance?

## References

Bandura, A. "Self-Efficacy: Toward a Unified Theory of Behavioral Change." *Psychological Review,* 1977, *84,* 191–215.

Berger, P. L., and Neuhaus, J. R. *To Empower People: The Role of Mediating Structures in Public Policy.* Washington, D.C.: American Enterprise Institute, 1977.

Brandstadter, J. "Personal and Social Control over Development: Some Implications of an Action Perspective in Life-Span Developmental Psychology." In P. B. Baltes and O. G. Brim, Jr. (eds.), *Life-Span Development and Behavior.* Vol. 6. San Diego, Calif.: Academic Press, 1984.

Brandstadter, J. "Individual Development in Social Action Contexts: Problems of Explanation." In J. Nesselroade and A. Von Eye (eds.), *Individual Development and Social Change: Explanatory Analysis.* San Diego, Calif.: Academic Press, 1985.

Brubaker, E. B. "Caring for a Dependent Spouse: Three Case Studies." *American Behavioral Scientist*, 1986, *29* (4), 485–496.

Collard, S., and Law, M. "The Limits of Perspective Transformation: A Critique of Mezirow's Theory." *Adult Education Quarterly*, 1989, *39* (2), 99–107.

Combs, A. W., Richards, A. C., and Richards, F. *Perceptual Psychology: A Humanistic Approach to the Study of Persons*. New York: HarperCollins, 1976.

Cook, J. R. "Citizen Response in a Neighborhood Under Threat." *American Journal of Community Psychology*, 1983, *11* (4), 459–471.

Datan, N. "Normative or Not? Confessions of a Fallen Epistemologist." *Life-Span Development Psychology: Nonnormative Life Events*. San Diego, Calif.: Academic Press, 1983.

Fendrich, J. M., and Krauss, E. S. "Student Activism and Adult Left-Wing Politics: A Causal Model of Political Socialization for Black, White and Japanese Students in the 1960s Generation." In L. Kreisberg (ed.), *Research in Social Movements: Conflicts and Change*. Vol. 1. Greenwich, Conn.: JAI Press, 1978.

Fishman, J. R., and Solomon, F. "Youth and Social Action: I. Perspectives on the Student Sit-in Movement." *American Journal of Orthopsychiatry*, 1963, *33* (5), 872–882.

Flacks, R. "Making History vs. Making Life: Dilemmas of an American Left." *Sociological Inquiry*, 1976, *46*, 263–280.

Fowler, J. *Stages of Faith*. New York: HarperCollins, 1981.

Frank, J. D., and Schonfield, J. "Commitment to Peace Work: II. A Closer Look at Determinants." *American Journal of Orthopsychiatry*, 1967, *37*, 112–119.

Freire, P. *Pedagogy of the Oppressed*. New York: Seabury Press, 1968.

Geschwender, B. N., and Geschwender, J. A. "Relative Deprivation and Participation in the Civil Rights Movement." *Social Science Quarterly*, 1973, *54*, 403–411.

Gilligan, C. *In a Different Voice: Psychological Theory of Women's Development*. Cambridge, Mass.: Harvard University Press, 1982.

Gore, P. M., and Rotter, J. B. "A Personality Correlate of Social Action." *Journal of Personality*, 1963, *31* (Mar.), 58–64.

Karp, D. A. "You Can Take the Boy Out of Dorchester, But You Can't Take Dorchester Out of the Boy: Toward a Social Psychology of Mobility." *Symbolic Interaction*, 1986, *9* (1), 19–36.

Kegan, R. *The Evolving Self: Problem and Process in Human Development*. Cambridge, Mass.: Harvard University Press, 1982.

Lachman, R., Lachman, J. L., and Butterfield, E. C. *Cognitive Psychology and Information Processing: An Introduction*. Hillsdale, N.J.: Erlbaum, 1979.

Ledrer, G. "Protest Movements as a Form of Political Action." In M. G. Hermann (ed.), *Political Psychology: Contemporary Problems and Issues*. San Francisco: Jossey-Bass, 1986.

Lerner, R. M., and Busch-Rossnagel, N. A. (eds.). *Individuals as Producers of Their Development*. San Diego, Calif.: Academic Press, 1981.

Lieberman, M. A. "Adaptive Processes in Late Life." In N. Datan and L. H. Ginsberg (eds.), *Life-Span Developmental Psychology: Normative Life Crises*. San Diego, Calif.: Academic Press, 1975.

McPhail, C. "Civil Disorder Participation: A Critical Examination of Recent Research." *American Sociological Review*, 1971, *36* (Dec.), 1058–1073.

Maidenberg, M., and Meyer, P. "The Berkeley Rebels Five Years Later: Has Age Mellowed the Pioneer Radicals?" *Detroit Free Press*, Feb. 1–7, 1970.

Mezirow, J. "A Critical Theory of Self-Directed Learning." In S. Brookfield (ed.), *Self-Directed Learning: From Theory to Practice*. New Directions for Continuing Education, no. 25. San Francisco: Jossey-Bass, 1985.

Mitchell, R. G., Jr. "Alienation and Deviance: Strain Theory Reconsidered." *Sociological Inquiry*, 1984, *54* (3), 330–345.

Nesselroade, J., and Von Eye, A. (eds.). *Individual Development and Social Change: Explanatory Analysis*. San Diego, Calif.: Academic Press, 1985.

Park, D. *Persons: Theories and Perceptions.* The Hague, Netherlands: Martinus Nijhoff, 1973.

Piaget, J. *The Construction of Reality in the Child.* New York: Basic Books, 1954.

Piven, F. F., and Cloward, R. A. *Poor People's Movements.* New York: Vintage, 1977.

Reese, H. W., and Smyer, M. A. "The Dimensionalization of Life Events." In E. J. Callahan and K. A. McCluskey (eds.), *Life-Span Developmental Psychology: Nonnormative Life Events.* San Diego, Calif.: Academic Press, 1983.

Runciman, W. G. *Relative Deprivation and Social Justice.* New York: Routledge & Kegan Paul, 1966.

Shingles, R. "Black Consciousness and Political Participation: The Missing Link." *American Political Science Review,* 1981, 75 (Mar.), 76–91.

Vanneman, R. D., and Pettigrew, T. F. "Race and Relative Deprivation in the Urban United States." *Race,* 1971, 13 (Apr.), 461–481.

Walsh, E. J., and Warland, R. H. "Social Movement Involvement in the Wake of a Nuclear Accident: Activists and Free Riders in the TMI Area." *American Sociological Review,* 1983, 48 (Dec.), 764–780.

Williams, R. L. "Finding Voice: The Transition from Individualism to Social Advocacy." Unpublished doctoral dissertation, Fielding Institute, Santa Barbara, Calif., 1989.

*ROBERT L. WILLIAMS is visiting assistant professor in the Pew Health Professions Program at the Institute for Policy Sciences and Public Affairs, Duke University, Durham, North Carolina. He is also a partner in Triangle Associates, a consulting firm in health care and education located in Chapel Hill, North Carolina.*

*The invention of the airplane offers a powerful example of independent learning that occurs outside the boundaries of institutional settings.*

# The Wright Brothers' Odyssey: Their Flight of Learning

*Lorraine A. Cavaliere*

In a letter to the noted American engineer, Octave Chanute, dated May 13, 1900, Wilbur Wright stated, "For some years I have been afflicted with the belief that flight is possible to man" (McFarland, 1972, p. 15). It was with this spirit and belief that the Wright brothers planned, developed, and completed one of the most vivid examples of a self-planned, self-directed adult learning project. This concept of the learning project was originally defined by Tough (1979), who conceptualized it as a "major, highly deliberate effort to gain certain knowledge and skill" (p. 1).

When the Wright brothers first articulated their dream of developing and flying a successful airplane, they began a process of independent learning that had a clearly defined goal. However, in the beginning, the steps and methods that would lead them to fulfilling their dream were merely that: a dream. These two individuals had no specific strategy planned or scientific map plotted that would serve as guidelines for their invention. Yet despite their lack of specific design and plan of action, on December 17, 1903, the Wrights achieved powered, sustained, controlled flight from level ground in their Flyer I at Kill Devil Hills in North Carolina. At that moment, the future of communications, transportation, education, and world affairs would begin to change significantly. These changes were effected by the independent, self-planned learning of two adults from Ohio, whose everyday business was the building and selling of bicycles. How did this happen, and what did they do to accomplish such a feat?

In order to answer this question, I conducted research that explored the behaviors the Wrights exhibited during their project. This case study was an attempt to explore their processes and patterns as a powerful example of independent learning that occurs outside of institutional settings. The definitive variables that characterize the concept of a learning project (Knowles, 1975; Tough, 1979; Brookfield, 1986) hold true for the Wrights' learning effort in that (1) it was a highly deliberate attempt to gain knowledge and skill; (2) it included affective changes as well as the development of cognitive and psychomotor skills; (3) the goals, learning decisions, location and use of resources, rate of progress, and method of evaluation were determined by the learner(s); and (4) there was no affiliation or assistance from a formal education system or institution.

The purpose of this chapter is to provide an analysis of the learning processes employed by the Wright brothers between 1875 and 1903; these enabled them to develop a heavier-than-air machine capable of sustained flight for the first time in the history of humankind. My research focused on the resource and communication networks that developed during the process of the Wrights' inventive project. Drawing on the literature of self-directed learning theory (Tough, 1979; Brookfield, 1986; Spear and Mocker, 1984) and social network theory (Luikart, 1977; Mitchell, 1969; Granovetter, 1973; Rogers and Kincaid, 1981; Crane, 1972), I charted the Wrights' learning behaviors and strategies using historical and biographical data bases from which I developed a learning process model.

## Their Odyssey: The Wrights' Learning Project

The early years of the Wright brothers within the context of an inquisitive family seem to have set the stage for the development of skills and personality traits that influenced their learning and led to the achievement of their objective. Born in 1867, Wilbur was the third child of Milton and Katharine Wright. Born four years after Wilbur (in 1871), Orville was the fourth of five children. There was a family history of a pioneering spirit, original thinking, and mechanical aptitude; and the brothers grew up in a home that encouraged the pursuit of intellectual curiosity (Crouch, 1981).

According to the historical documents, one of the initial resources that engaged their interest was a toy, the Penoud helicopter, which was given to them by their father in 1878, when Orville was seven and Wilbur was eleven. They played with this model and built larger replications to test but were unsuccessful in achieving flight. This early skill development would prove most influential during their efforts to invent the airplane.

Their formal schooling ended with the completion of high school, although they never formally graduated. In 1899, at the ages of thirty-two and twenty-eight, they began a serious pursuit of their dream. They were mature adults with family responsibilities (although neither married), and both were charged with the management of a full-time business. Though their life circumstances were ordinary and modest, they had the desire and found the time to strive to attain their goal. Their work habits were established at an early age to incorporate organization, thoroughness, attention to detail, problem-solving tactics, inquisitiveness, and mechanical tinkering. These habits and skills, a clear objective, and an environment that encouraged them laid the foundation for their success. These family and personality traits of curiosity, problem-solving ability, persistence, and innovativeness are characteristics of successful adult learners identified by Roe (1953), Gross (1982), and Houle (1984).

The Wrights' odyssey was a classic learning adventure paralleling the journey of Odysseus, the Greek hero, in his attempt to reach home after the siege of Troy. The Wrights and Odysseus both understood their final goal. Both were propelled by the winds and the whims of fortune: their routes were determined by circumstances and by context, decisions were made en route, and they met seemingly insurmountable obstacles along the way. Yet the environment and the context offered information and resources, and persistence remained their ally throughout their journey.

The Wrights, acting as problem solvers during the process of their learning project, exhibited repetitive core categories of learning behaviors similar to those cited by Henry (1960), Brookfield (1986) and Oddi (1987). These behaviors of modeling, concept construction, reading, observing, discussion, contemplating, planning, experimenting, using trial and error, practicing, and comparing and contrasting were continuous and cyclical throughout the learning project.

Incidents of specific learning behaviors provided a map of the progress of the Wrights' learning project. The beginning and end points of the journey were defined, and the specific behaviors that were employed throughout the project were identified. However, the stages of their journey toward flight were yet to be discovered. The map of their journey had been drawn, but it contained no topography or established routes of travel. This layer of information, termed *basic cognitive processes,* emerged as a result of the expectation levels set by the Wrights and their reaction to failure. Just as Odysseus planned his specific steps home as the voyage progressed, each day of the Wrights' learning journey consisted of the same sequence of basic cognitive processes: goal setting (What is our destination today?); focusing (What route will be best?); persevering (How far must we travel to reach the day's destination?); reformulating (How must our plans change?). Each day the journey creates changes due to contextual forces that affect it. Individual learning behaviors occur simultaneously and continuously throughout the journey (that is, the traveler is always engaging in some mode of learning behavior: observing, discussion, pondering, or comparing).

As their learning journey unfolded, five distinct stages became apparent. During each of them, the same four basic repetitive cognitive processes (goal setting, focusing, persevering, and reformulating) occurred. Each stage ended with a clearly identifiable breakpoint, preceded by frustration and confusion on the part of the Wright brothers. Each stage was separated by a period of disengagement, and each was characterized by a different aspect of the basic problem-solving processes identified by major learning theories related to inquiry and performance (Houle, 1984). These stages gained in momentum as they neared their goals. The labels for each stage characterize the general focus of activity and describe the level of intensity of the learning project at these various stages: (1) inquiring, (2) modeling, (3) experimenting and practicing, (4) theorizing and perfecting, and (5) actualizing.

**Inquiring.** The Wrights began their self-planned learning project to solve the problems of manned flight. This problem-solving orientation to self-planned learning was noted by Knowles (1973) and Penland (1977). The mechanism triggering their launch into this project was the sudden death of Otto Lilienthal, the famous German gliding enthusiast. (In the summer of 1896, Lilienthal stalled and fell to his death from an altitude of fifty feet while flying his glider.) Lilienthal had captured the imagination and admiration of the Wright brothers through his daring experiments detailed in newspaper accounts published around the world. The motivating effect of Lilienthal's death on the Wrights concurs with Spear and Mocker (1984) and Brookfield (1986), who contend that a decision to engage in a learning project with a specific goal is usually preceded by some change in life circumstance or some calamitous event that induces exploration and problem solving.

The first action taken in their learning project was a search for books on flight, "but they found little beyond a few volumes on ornithology and never too trustworthy or detailed news accounts" (Crouch, 1981, p. 227). The Wrights began an intensive search for existing written materials on the current progress toward the solution of the problem of flight. Their initial efforts at reading books began with resources in the Dayton Library and expanded to communications with the Smithsonian Institution. They read the works of many of the leading aviation experts of that time, including Lilienthal, Langley, and Chanute. After extensive reading, the Wrights realized that what was known was insignificant to their learning goal.

**Modeling.** The lack of information in the literature piqued their curiosity further and spurred them to engage in hours of observations of bird flight. Lilienthal's gliding experiments also acted as a guide for them in the construction and flying of kites.

This stage involved use of existing information and formats of experimentation for the Wrights to emulate in their efforts to discover flight. During this phase, they modeled previous efforts by others and in so doing discovered that machines built to that point and their underlying concepts were incorrect. This process provided an opportunity to repeat past performance and to compare and contrast information.

The use and refinement of a single model (paradigm) proved to be one reason why they were successful—as opposed to others experimenting with multiple design configurations. They stayed with Lillienthal's basic designs and continually refined the model based on feedback from experiments and flight failures.

**Experimenting and Practicing.** After these initial learning behaviors of reading, observation, and model construction, they began experimentation processes with their kites and model gliders. The information obtained from experiments about wing shape, control, and stability was valuable to their growing understanding of flight; however, they reached a plateau in their own ability to explore further the scientific variables. It was at this point—in 1900, as their plans for their first full-scale model were taking shape—that Wilbur decided to make contact with Octave Chanute. This decision was based on their need to acquire information that they could not discover through their own experimentation and observation. They knew Octave Chanute was an international aviation expert and could also be a conduit to other individuals and groups pursuing the goal to invent the first airplane.

The pattern of external contacts made by the Wright brothers indicate the most frequently contacted and utilized resource was Chanute, and only seventeen contacts were initiated during the four-year duration of the communication network that formed during their project. Their primary reason for making contact was to obtain information. Whenever their need for information became greater than their personal resources, the Wrights got in touch with external resources. The information obtained usually proved incorrect, insufficient, or irrelevant; it did not seem either to advance or deter their progress. Yet these contacts did act as a feedback mechanism, providing cognitive parameters that the Wrights could use to modify and regulate their subsequent actions.

External information sources merely provided starting points and frames of reference from which they could compare and contrast their own experimental results. The acquisition of the experimental data was a result of their careful observations, measurements, and note taking about each trial flight—everything from models in the wind tunnel to full-scale models at Kitty Hawk. These results affected the choice of learning behaviors more directly than the basic cognitive processes employed.

The Wrights believed that practice would ensure their success. Skill development through practice and repetition would lead to freedom from controlled, conscious body movements and the cognitive processing necessary in the beginning stages of mastery. This freedom would occur because the conscious efforts become part of the unconscious psyche and the skills needed to control an airplane become second nature. At this point, they as pilots could begin to demonstrate the "art" of flying: interpreting, theorizing, being innovative and creating. (For example, piano playing and dancing can reach a level of improvisation and complex integration only once basic skills are mastered through repetition and practice.)

This level of mastery is the gateway to the breakthroughs that occur when the whole picture or outcome, rather than basic skills, becomes the focus.

**Theorizing and Perfecting.** By 1902, the basic model that the Wrights had developed and refined through experimentation and practice was at the point of being airworthy. Their ability to fly the machine was also at a place where they could control the craft and make deductions about errors in the performance of the pilots and the machine. It was during this stage that their initial hypotheses were proven, and the three problems of control, airfoil design, and power source were solved. Through numerous refinements of the basic model, they had now perfected their skill and their machine. At this level, the individual skills had been combined with cognitive understanding.

**Actualizing.** By 1903, the Wrights realized their work had progressed farther than that of others in the field. This realization was based upon the external and internal feedback they had been receiving from their contacts and from their own experiments. Information received at this point completed the learning cycle. As the holders of the information power base, the Wrights' sense of where they were in relation to others seemed to act as an intense impetus or motivation for the action that would finally fulfill their initial goal. And their final act—the achievement of flight—represented a paradigm shift, a scientific revolution, that demonstrates the power of individual learning efforts.

## Influence of the Context on Learning

The context in which an event manifests itself is often as important in describing and explaining the phenomenon as the event itself. Based upon the analysis of this case study, the contextual framework for the learning project appears to control much of the decision making employed by the adult learner. And the Wrights' work did not progress in isolation. The biographical background indicates that the two brothers were in constant communication. In addition, they kept in regular contact with the leader of the informal information network of the time, Octave Chanute, who channeled information to and from an international aeronautical network.

The Wrights' network was formed for a specific purpose and functioned only for so long as the Wrights needed information. As soon as the problems were solved, they disconnected themselves from these ties. But the network provided the Wright brothers with information, support, and a reading as to where their progress stood relative to their peer group. The importance of this network to the Wrights' work demonstrates how voluntary organizations and informal learning networks can assist learning. This finding is similar to that of Luikart (1977) and Beder, Darkenwald, and Valentine (1983).

As we have seen, the information needed to solve the mystery of flight was not obtained from external resources. The three critical puzzle pieces of control, airfoil design, and power source were solved solely through the ingenuity of the Wrights. The solutions to these problems came after a series of specific behaviors were employed by the Wrights. This result supports the conceptual construct of the organizing circumstance presented by Spear and Mocker (1984), contending that the learning project is structured from limited alternatives within the learner's environment. Technology had advanced to a point where the cognitive and material resources provided excellent timing for this event to occur. Had the Wrights attempted this feat fifty years sooner, the technological advances in materials and engineering, as well as the consolidation of existing information, would not have been available (Kuhn, [1962] 1970).

Their learning project took place exclusively outside of any institutional setting, without direct institutional support (for example, information, money, and technical resources). This context for learning concurs with the findings of Penland (1977), Houle (1984), Tough (1979), and Gross (1982), who indicate that the most favored locations for learning were the home and the workplace, which in the Wrights' case were one and the same.

## The Power of the Odyssey: Learning in Flight

This case study of the learning journey of the Wright brothers vividly depicts the power of personal learning. This type of learning has the power to change dramatically the individual and society at large. This study also illustrates specific forces within the learner and the learning environment that propel the learning project along the path of progress. These forces I refer to as power variables. They clearly affect the learning process and emanate from both internal and external sources.

A number of power variables were exhibited by the Wright brothers: feedback, information, persistence, practice, reflection, timing, intuition, failure, and momentum—as well as the powers of the mentor, the model, and the partner—exerted a directional force upon the learners and their project that deserves further study and research.

For example, the power of a partnership to provide feedback and motivation was a dynamic force at work during the progress of the Wright brothers' project. The Wrights worked as a team, complementing their unique strengths and weaknesses. They labored, experimented, discussed, pondered, argued, and succeeded together. As partners, they served as mirrors, sources of reflection from whom feedback was received to reformulate ideas and broaden perspectives. As partners, they served as mutual helpers through verbal exchanges and mental probes. The power and dynamics of collaborative work could spawn a variety of research themes.

The force of the power of information is illustrated by the observation that its flow is directed by those holding the information power base—

those with the most recent and unique bits of information. People in need of information become aware of who has it and can initiate a request. Information is therefore pulled through the network by those in need of data, rather than being pushed by those who have it. This position of power relative to movement within a resource network seems to be a potent ingredient to understanding what motivates the learner to act and what moves information through a system. These interpretations compare favorably with the research of Whitten and Wolfe (1974), who focused on the processes and forces moving people and information within networks.

In summary, the invention of the airplane was the end of a learning journey for the Wright brothers and the beginning of an odyssey of flight for the world that followed. The story of their personal odyssey illustrated that the behaviors exhibited by the Wrights in their learning project were repetitive, forming series, groups, and stages of action. Their behaviors were nonlinear, with the learners demonstrating increased proficiency as they moved through their project. The productive outcomes of their collaborative teamwork and synergy were driven by the cyclical forces of goal setting, feedback, and motivation. Although their long-range goal was clear, the planning and goal setting that took place in the learning project was contingent on contextual circumstances and feedback. This feedback provided one form of motivation for their continued efforts to complete the learning project successfully. Their involvement in the formal information network motivated their actions as well. This case study thus demonstrates that self-directed learning does not occur in isolation and that defined goals can be accomplished through practice and perseverance.

## References

Beder, H., Darkenwald, G. G., and Valentine, T. "Self-Planned Professional Learning Among Public School Adult Education Directors: A Social Network Analysis." In *Proceedings of the Twenty-Fourth Annual Adult Education Research Conference,* no. 24. Montreal, Canada: Concordia University/University of Montreal, 1983.

Brookfield, S. D. *Understanding and Facilitating Adult Learning: A Comprehensive Analysis of Principles and Effective Practices.* San Francisco: Jossey-Bass, 1986.

Crane, D. *Invisible Colleges: Diffusion of Knowledge in Scientific Communities.* Chicago: University of Chicago Press, 1972.

Crouch, T. D. *A Dream of Wings: Americans and the Airplane, 1875–1905.* New York: Norton, 1981.

Granovetter, M. S. "The Strength of Weak Ties." *American Journal of Sociology,* 1973, 1360–1380.

Gross, R. *The Independent Scholar's Handbook.* Reading, Mass.: Addison-Wesley, 1982.

Henry, J. "A Cross-Cultural Outline of Education." *Current Anthropology,* 1960, *1,* 267–305.

Houle, C. O. *Patterns of Learning: New Perspectives on Life-Span Education.* San Francisco: Jossey-Bass, 1984.

Knowles, M. S. *The Adult Learner: A Neglected Species.* Houston, Tex.: Gulf Publishing, 1973.

Knowles, M. S. *Self-Directed Learning: A Guide for Learners and Teachers.* Chicago: Association Press, 1975.

Kuhn, T. S. *The Structure of Scientific Revolutions.* Chicago: University of Chicago Press, 1970. (Originally published 1962.)

Luikart, C. *Social Networks and Self-Planned Adult Learning.* Chapel Hill, N.C.: University of North Carolina Press, 1977.

McFarland, M. W. (ed.). *The Papers of Wilbur and Orville Wright: 1899–1905.* Vol. 1. New York: Arno Press, 1972.

Mitchell, J. C. "The Concept and Use of Social Networks." In J. C. Mitchell (ed.), *Social Networks in Urban Situations.* Manchester, England: Manchester University Press, 1969.

Oddi, L. F. "Perspectives on Self-Directed Learning." *Adult Education Quarterly,* 1987, *38* (1), 21–31.

Penland, P. R. *Self-Planned Learning in America.* Pittsburgh, Penn.: Book Center, University of Pittsburgh, 1977.

Roe, A. *The Making of a Scientist.* New York: Dodd, Mead, 1953.

Rogers, E. M., and Kincaid, D. L. *Communication Networks.* New York: Free Press, 1981.

Spear, G. E., and Mocker, D. W. "The Organizing Circumstances: Environmental Determinants in Self-Directed Learning." *Adult Education Quarterly,* 1984, *35* (1), 1–10.

Tough, A. *The Adult's Learning Projects: A Fresh Approach to Theory and Practice in Adult Learning.* Research in Education Series, no. 1. Toronto, Canada: Ontario Institute for Studies in Education, 1979.

Whitten, N. E., Jr., and Wolfe, A. W. "Network Analyses." In J. J. Honigmann (ed.), *Handbook of Social and Cultural Anthropology.* Skokie, Ill.: Rand McNally, 1974.

*LORRAINE A. CAVALIERE is director of continuing studies at Rutgers University. She is a member of The Ninety Nines: International Organization of Women Pilots.*

*This chapter argues for greater emphasis on a process orientation to adult learning, on nonverbal means of communication, and on the value of intuitive knowledge. Learning in modern dance is offered as a possible model for change.*

# Let's Face the Music and Dance: A View of Learning in the Arts

*Angela Sgroi*

> All the disasters of mankind, all the misfortunes that histories are so full of, the blunders of politicians, the miscarriages of great commanders—all this comes from want of skill in dancing.
> —Jean Baptist Poquelin, *Molière*

Adults of all ages and backgrounds can be found in any community, in a variety of settings, coming together or working independently in the serious creation or performance of some art work. Active participation in the arts seems to have special value to many adults. Thus, we have community choirs, regional theater companies and orchestras, and local art exhibits. The Out and About arts-education program for retired citizens in Vermont has produced artists who have won prizes, sold art work, and been published. In Washington, D.C., there is a company called Dancers of the Third Age, made up of older men and women who had been active in many walks of life before their retirement. They did not see themselves as artists before they joined the company, and now they are performing concerts and giving workshops to professional dancers throughout the United States and abroad.

More famous examples of this phenomenon are Alexander Borodin, a chemist by profession, a well-known composer by avocation; Frank O'Connor, the librarian who wrote some of the best short stories in Irish literature; and Helen Houvan Santmeyer, a woman in her eighties, who in 1985 published her first novel, *And Ladies of the Club*. She had been a housewife all of her life and had worked on her novel at odd moments for over fifty years.

What do all of these individuals have in common? There are two

NEW DIRECTIONS FOR ADULT AND CONTINUING EDUCATION, no. 53, Spring 1992 © Jossey-Bass Publishers

things: they have a nonartistic means of making their livelihood, and they practice an art form. They see their art as an avocation; they are amateurs who participate for the love of the art.

The type of learning, especially adult learning, that takes place in the arts has not been the focus of much research. Nevertheless, practitioners and proponents of the arts have strongly encouraged arts education for a long time. They point to the broadening effect that this kind of learning has on a person's life.

Abraham Maslow (1968) writes: "Creative art education . . . may be especially important not so much for turning out artists or art products, as for turning out better people . . . who are able confidently to face tomorrow not knowing . . . what will happen, with confidence enough . . . to improvise in that situation which has never existed before" (p. 4).

Very little about avocational artistic learning is documented. However, even so, some patterns have begun to emerge that shed light on this sometimes elusive kind of learning.

Education in present U.S. society moves primarily along three paths to learning: it is product-oriented; it uses a verbal means of communication; and it relies on scientific method and rational thinking for obtaining knowledge. These paths most accurately reflect the driving forces in our society and are thus appropriate in assisting people to attain success. At the same time, however, there is a tendency to rely on them too much and to neglect other important means of learning.

For adults who study modern dance, the desire to develop other ways of understanding their world is an important factor in choosing to participate and some of the research seems to show that this is true for learners in any art form (Halsted, 1981; Kaltoft, 1990; and Rugh, 1990). Learning in the arts focuses on a process orientation, develops nonverbal communication skills, and fosters a reliance on intuitive knowledge. Since my own work has been done on adults who study modern dance seriously, this research will be used to describe a possible model through which learning in other art forms can be viewed.

What is learning in modern dance? Is it different from learning in other, more typical, kinds of adult learning? What implications does that difference have for all educators of adults? This chapter will describe the learning transaction in modern dance, explain how it helps a person develop alternative paths to learning, and recommend ways in which adult educators can incorporate process orientation, nonverbal communication, and intuitive knowledge into other adult education contexts.

## Fascination with the Art Form

To understand fully the teaching-learning transaction in learning modern dance, the reader must first understand something about what it is that draws people to learn it. It starts with the art form itself and the learners' love of and fascination with dance.

**What Modern Dance Is.** The first time a person attends a dance concert, she or he is confronted with the first reality of dance (and all of the performing arts): it is all in the present. Beiswanger (1970) says that "dancing is always a process of becoming—everything in the dance is for the first time" (p. 84).

According to Joyce (1973), the elements of dance are body, force, space, and time. For Joyce, the element of body includes, "Body parts— outer parts, such as head, shoulders, rib cage, hips, back, arms, hands, legs, and feet; and inner parts, such as heart, lungs, muscles, bones, and joints. . . . Body moves—such as stretching and bending, twisting and circling, lifting and collapsing, swinging, swaying, and shaking . . . [and] steps . . . walk, run, leap, hop, skip, gallop, slide" (pp. 2–3). Space includes the shape one makes even when not moving, level, direction, size, focus, place, and pathway; and "all movement can be altered by changes in force" (p. 4). Finally, the element of time includes the underlying beat or pulse of a movement, as well as speed, duration, and the combination of these elements into rhythmic patterns.

A review of the history of modern dance reveals that many of the most shocking and radical innovations resulted from a questioning of the traditional uses and definitions of space and time, as well as concepts of the human body. For example, choreographers of the Judson Church Movement of the 1960s changed the concept of space by disregarding the obstacles on stage that blocked part of the dance from view and performing in nontraditional spaces (such as Twyla Tharp's "Medley," done in Central Park; Trisha Brown's "Roof Piece," performed on the top of a building; and Merideth Monks' "Juice," done in an art museum) (Livet, 1978).

These innovations eventually make their way into modern dance classes. Teachers of dance use these concepts frequently to create images for their students. Murray Louis (1980) speaks as a dancer and a teacher when he says, "The space surrounding the dancer becomes his canvas. He can draw upon it and define it in many ways. The space inside his body allows him to give texture and quality to movement" (p. 153).

Similarly, he addresses the concept of time: "The time he [the dancer] employs can range from the pulse of the heartbeat to the most exacting syncopations, to the denial of time altogether" (p. 153). Doris Humphrey's dramatic "Water Study," created in 1928, uses the unison breathing of the dancers as accompaniment and meter for the movement.

The body has also been treated in nontraditional and experimental ways. Alwin Nikolais, for example, uses dancers' bodies in a way that expresses erotic themes in one dance ("Foreplay"); yet in other dances he disguises or otherwise obliterates the human form entirely through the use of lighting and sets ("Temple"; "Scenario") or costume (a dance in which dancers are completely encased in bags) (Livet, 1978).

Each modern dance style has its own set of values and philosophy upon which its movement is based. Since most modern dance teachers of adult students have been trained in at least one of the major modern dance traditions, it is the philosophy of the instructor that is usually communicated.

**Why Modern Dance Fascinates.** Adult learners choose modern dance for many reasons, but the major driving force is simply their love of and fascination with the art form. It is beautiful to watch and to do, and it "speaks" in a way that nothing else can.

When they dance, they appreciate it with their body and mind, their senses and sensibilities. In fact, this combination seems to be one of the things that draws them to dance. One dancer explains the excitement she feels when the teacher choreographs particularly well for class: "She gives us a basic combination, and then she adds a little something here and a little something there, constantly making it more intricate and intellectually interesting to watch and move through" (Kitty, an adult dancer). This union of the physical and mental in dance is fundamental.

## The Nature of Learning Modern Dance

The art form defines not only the content of the learning, but its process, as well as, perhaps, the type of person who chooses to learn it.

**Developing and Learning in a New Way.** Adult amateur dancers have said that they were seeking something for themselves; they selected modern dance (some say that it selected them); and now they must learn how it is done—how thoughts and feelings are translated into movement. They must discover how to make the magic, for that is how the dancers often view the learning.

Part of the fascination with learning modern dance is that it is significantly different from the kind of learning they have experienced most of their lives. They feel they are developing different aspects of themselves: "I hate my job right now. It's very logical, step-by-step. I'm a business administrator. . . . When someone does a [dance] combination, I see the whole thing . . . so I'm using a whole different way of visualizing and conceptualizing" (Helen).

Again, the focus on the interweaving of the physical and intellectual in dance yields a greatly heightened sense of awareness. Dancers learn to control their bodies by using mental images as well as physical exercises. They find that a new avenue of communication and expression has been opened to them. As Barnes (1969) advises, "Actions, they say, speak louder than words, louder and truer. When people dance, they dance naked in their spirits" (p. 267).

A thirty-year-old business woman finds that the opportunities for expression in dance hold a particular lure for her: "I'm very successful in the business world, and I've never given myself the time to develop anything artistic. . . . I have really come to a time in my life where I'm developing that other side of the brain, and I'm blossoming."

Joyce's goal (1973) is to help her students to communicate through movement. She has found that her students learn to "see the elements of dance in the world and find they can relate to and communicate about what they see and hear and feel. They develop and use their kinesthetic sense. They perceive themselves. They know their size, their strength, their timing; they are aware of movement control and flow. They can speak 'body language' and can read it in others" (p. 8).

Learning in dance, and learning in all the arts, helps people to see their world in new ways. In her research with adult painting students, Halsted (1981) found: "Despite the fact that new students come to class 'wanting a picture,' and despite a limiting technical procedure which many teachers impose in order to accomplish that goal, something happens during the art process which demands more of them . . . and students gain in aesthetic awareness from painting classes. All students report heightened awareness of nature, a curiosity about other art work" (pp. 139-140).

The aesthetic quality of dance, as in all other arts, is based upon the creative use of form within time and space. This form cannot exist without control. Almost all of the time in dance classes is spent learning about control in some way, developing physical strength and agility, as well as learning to use imagery to influence the quality of movement. At the same time, the dancer must also discover how to let go, to flow with the spirit of the movement. The key to accomplishing learning in all of these areas is to develop skill through a fully integrated mind-body involvement, which requires complete concentration. This total immersion temporarily frees the mind from literal thinking, problems, and stresses of the day and involves the dancer more in the practice of the art.

In general, an intuitive approach to knowing is developed. In addition to learning to see in new ways, dancers must judge their own movement by relying on its feel, as well as on teacher feedback, as they cannot see themselves.

Thinking differently and seeing the aesthetic quality of work in class are an important part of the learning that is specific to modern dance and other art forms. The word *quality* is commonly used and always in the same way: to refer to the overall pattern, feeling, and spirit of a dance or movement sequence.

**Process Orientation of Dance.** Again, the learning follows the nature of the art form. Like dance itself, its learning involves "a process of becoming" (Beiswanger, 1970, p. 84).

Something that must be understood about learning modern dance—or any performance-oriented, artistic dancing—is that taking class is a major part of dancing for professionals and amateurs alike. The instrument (the body) must be constantly maintained and improved. Professional dancers are in class four to five hours a day when they are not rehearsing or performing. For those who wish to continue actively dancing, even as amateurs, taking class never really ends.

Most adult amateur dancers dance throughout their lives. Conversations with older dancers from Washington, D.C., helped clarify this fact because they were able to describe their involvement in dance over their lifetimes. They report having stopped dancing for perhaps ten or twenty years before they returned to it, but they saw this as only a temporary hiatus in their lifelong involvement.

The behaviors that characterize learning in modern dance seem to cluster into two modes of involvement: overcoming barriers and engaging. There are often physical and psychological barriers of some kind that adults who choose to study modern dance must overcome. Physical barriers might be injury and pain, illness, and the restrictive effects on movement of an aging body. Psychological and emotional barriers are sometimes more difficult to overcome than the physical barriers. Perhaps the most common barrier is the feeling of insecurity and even fear about doing something that one is not very good at. Gloria (who is 49) says, "I am convinced that I'm too old to be here with kids. I'm much too fat to be running around in a leotard. . . . It's not comfortable. I don't feel capable. I have to convince myself that it's OK for me to do this." She never misses a class.

Engaging is the actual involvement in the learning. It means going to class, if not always religiously, then with commitment; listening and following the teacher, even submitting to the teacher's guidance; thinking; self-teaching; pushing through the difficult movement; evaluating progress; and extending the learning outside of class.

The learners studied made a commitment to themselves to learn dance, so their involvement in the activity is resolute. One dancer never participated in the arts before she started to dance. She commented, "I'm committed . . . no matter what it is. . . . I make sure I get home on time for that class. I think I missed it once during the stock market crash [of 1987]."

Even when they relinquish control and submit to the teacher, the dance students are thinking about and controlling what they learn. It is as if they rely on a self-teaching style as much as on the teacher. The teacher often runs the class in such a way as to push students through a difficult combination. They also push themselves.

Evaluation is an extremely important part of the learning process for adult dancers. Monitoring of progress is frequent and varied; correction and feedback from the teacher are a must for most dancers (as discussed below). External indications of the dancers' learning progress are such things as awards and concert performances. Since most studios do not organize a performance, one group of adult dance students researched, choreographed, produced, and performed their own public concert (they called themselves the Independent Choreographers).

Their own self-evaluation is constant and critical. In addition to external measures, the dancers will assess their progress against some internal objective that is somehow identified by "feel." One of the dancers, Evelyn, says things like, "That still feels kind of clumsy. There are parts of the class that still feel not there." Clearly, "there" is some quantity that exists only inside of Evelyn. Yet she implies that it is clear to her when she attains it. Another dancer remarks, "The movement could be more full. . . . It's an inhibition that you feel then in your movement. . . . So it's gone like two centimeters deeper. It's not there yet. But it's shifting" (Helen).

## The Learning-Teaching Interaction

There is a give-and-take between the teacher and the learners in these dance classes that seems to enrich the experiences of both.

**The Adult Student.** The adult learners of modern dance know themselves and their learning styles, and they are decisive about what they choose to learn. They decide what it is that they are interested in, and they go decisively about selecting the place, the time, and the teacher; deciding what they will or will not learn; and, even, choosing to temporarily relinquish control to someone else. They choose modern dance because it "fits."

**The Good Teacher.** Ultimately, the class reflects the teacher. The dancers' responses to teachers, both good and bad, have been the strongest and most pervasive elements in the research.

Adult dancers are very clear about what makes the "good" teacher. The good teacher has full knowledge of modern dance and of teaching it, has respect and high expectations for adult students, works with the whole person, inspires trust, and has a powerful influence.

The power and importance of correction and positive feedback cannot be overstated. Students expect and appreciate it. One adult dancer, Rich, explained that one way he evaluated Roz (a teacher) was that she paid a great deal of attention to individual students and cared about their progress. Another dancer, Evelyn, said, "Actually, for me it's positive reinforcement because it shows that I'm being noticed and that I'm worth being noticed." Laura said, "I felt special when she corrected me. . . . I felt like I was worthy of being corrected, and that was a really good feeling." Laura's further explanation is perhaps a little more romantic but provides additional clarification: "I feel loved, that's all. I don't care how I dance. . . . It's because she's responding to me. . . . When you're a dancer, you want someone to respond to you. I don't care whether it's dancing or what it is. It's just that someone is responding to your being . . . in a total way. She's absolutely there."

The bad teacher, in contrast, is described as "condescending" and lacking in respect for students. "It's just that Melissa [a teacher] has a . . . holdout personality. . . . That's why with Melissa, I felt so dead. There was a nonpresence, a nonbeing. . . . I knew that my body was not dancing for this woman" (Laura).

Teaching techniques most employed in the dance class are careful pacing to keep the dancers moving, the use of imagery, pushing the dancers to continue doing difficult combinations, repetition, and musical support. The open space of the studio provides the proper setting for the movement of the dance class.

**The Interaction.** Modern dance is not something that can be entirely self-taught. The learner must receive instruction from a teacher. Anyone can attend dance concerts, read about dance, and talk to experts about modern dance to learn to appreciate the art form. But learning to dance can only be done with someone who knows it: "You are their clay. . . . It's the ultimate romantic sort of teacher-pupil relationship because you work for them. You make your body do anything for them" (Laura). Thus, on the one hand, there can be an intense, loyal attachment to a (trusted) teacher to whom the learner has relinquished control. The attachment is not always made, but, when it is, the influence of the teacher is very strong. On the other hand, the adult learner is in control. If there is one sure thing about the learning patterns of the adults, it is that they make the decisions. This is pervasive throughout the adult education literature (see Knowles, 1970; Brookfield, 1986; Brockett and Hiemstra, 1991). This tension between control and deference defines the nature of the teaching-learning interaction for adults who study modern dance.

The adult learners submit to the teacher's expert guidance for several reasons: for the specialized knowledge of a visual medium, for a structured dance experience, for the discipline necessary to dance, for leadership in perfecting the art and the craft, and for correction from someone with an artistic sensibility.

In the give-and-take of the interaction, the teacher learns from the student. A critical discovery for teachers who work with the elderly Dancers of the Third Age is the need for a consistent focus on serious artistic goals at all levels of activity, despite the ages of the dancers. This focus requires that the choreographers and teachers (usually younger, professional dancers) must first broaden their perspectives in dance to "see" the beauty and expression in the movements of older people. Without condescending, the choreographer or teacher must use the particular strengths of each dancer. Lerman (1984), artistic director, explains: "If the classes are to succeed, a teacher must respond to the beauty and capability of each student. This acceptance is not difficult to do, since the dances of these students are, in fact, beautiful. If teachers have stereotyped ideas of what graceful, pretty, or expressive movement is, then they will have to change.

Any preconceived notion of perfect form will get in the way of seeing the senior adult dancers for what they are capable of doing" (p. 6).

This notion of finding inherent beauty in the movement of older dancers is the key to Lerman's work and represents her contribution to the art of modern dance. She has found a different form of grace and beauty in the movements of older people and is keenly aware of the unique expressions that only people with experience can convey; she is able to demonstrate these insights to others through her choreography and to help other dancer-teachers to see and work with it in their own older dancers.

## Using Learning in the Arts to Cultivate the Art of Teaching

I will never forget the first time that I began reading on my own, when everything came together for me, and the words formed sentences that actually held meaning. There was an incredible surge of power from that learning, something that can never be adequately described. This experience might provide a clue to what adult educators are looking for. There is magic not only in learning to unlock the mysteries of art making, but in unlocking any mysteries in life. Perhaps the contribution this chapter can make to educators is to suggest a way of learning that might help reveal this process of unlocking a mystery and exploring the "art" in teaching.

How does one bring art into teaching? Where is the mystery in basic skills and literacy education? What magic is needed to unlock those mysteries, if found?

Bringing the art into teaching means, in part, looking for the beautiful, the mysterious, the excitement of the subject—and loving it. In literacy and basic skills, there is the beauty and joy of language or the wonder of numbers. Part of the teacher's job is knowing these wonders, loving them personally, and passing that knowledge and feeling along to learners.

It also means remembering that learning is not only a product; it is primarily a process, especially for adult educators who espouse the notion that learning is lifelong and that an important goal of education is helping people to learn how to learn. Teachers can look for opportunities to incorporate a process orientation into everything that learners are asked to do. It is a matter of changing the focus of activities.

This is not a new idea. Most discussions of methodology for learners from three to one hundred years old encourage this approach. Instead of focusing on the finished product, emphasize the steps along the way. Have students record (perhaps in journals) and evaluate their process. Even though our professional literature is full of such suggestions, most formal classroom situations at all levels still focus on the product. Recent examples of research and applications of such a focus in the workplace can be found in the work of Marsick (1987) and Zeph (1991).

Bringing the art into teaching means remembering that learning is not only achieved through verbal modes of communication, but also through all of the nonverbal means. Teachers might look for ways to include nonverbal modes of communication into whatever is their particular subject. Can ideas be represented graphically, communicated through movement, the playing of roles, or mime? Can literature or other works of art be used to discuss topics or themes of importance in your teaching?

Bringing the art into teaching means remembering that knowledge is not only what we know through scientific investigation or rational thought, but also what we know intuitively. This undertaking might be more difficult. Obtaining knowledge through the use of intuition is usually the creative process in any work, even in scientific work.

If we take the advice of arts educators and philosophers, we would continually seek opportunities to encourage creative thinking in the learning process because it is "sometimes . . . a transcendence of self. . . . [There is universally] reported a seeing of formerly hidden truth, a revelation in the strict sense, a stripping away of veils, and finally, almost always, the whole experience is experienced as bliss, ecstasy, rapture, exaltation" (Maslow, 1968, p. 6).

For adult educators, McLeish's (1976) less abstract description might be more useful: "The word central to the individual person involved . . . is preparation: preparation of mood, of attack with one's resources upon a fascinating problem, and along with that, preparation of skills and competence to handle the [creative] 'visitation' when it occurs. Thus, the tides of invention which constantly flooded Mozart with the seemingly effortless music on travels . . . were part of the process of a human being whose whole life was one of readiness and attunement to musical composition. . . . But . . . the mysterious arrival came to a conscious mind already stretched to create, or exhausted or quiescent after days of striving" (p. 44).

Like McLeish, Fine (1980) has little difficulty in an analytic approach to the creative process and to pervasive feelings of ecstasy and transcendence: "Inspiration should be taken out of the class of magical devices and returned to its normal role in human affairs as another aspect of healthy functioning which is open to everybody and which can even be taught" (p. 1216).

These ways of bringing the art into teaching are not always easily accomplished. In the end, perhaps the most valuable gift that teachers give learners is the inspiration and encouragement to learn. Teachers who give these gifts successfully do it by endowing their students with a part of themselves.

## References

Barnes, C. "Dance." In L. Kroneberger (ed.), Quality: Its Image in the Arts. New York: Atheneum, 1969.

Beiswanger, G. "Chance and Design in Choreography." In M. H. Nadel and C. G. Nadel (eds.), The Dance Experience: Readings in Dance Appreciation. New York: Praeger, 1970.

Brockett, R. G., and Hiemstra, R. *Self-Direction in Adult Learning: Perspectives on Theory, Research, and Practice.* London and New York: Routledge, 1991.

Brookfield, S. D. *Understanding and Facilitating Adult Learning: A Comprehensive Analysis of Principles and Effective Practices.* San Francisco: Jossey-Bass, 1986.

Fine, R. "Work, Depression, and Creativity: Psychoanalytic Perspective." *Psychological Reports,* 1980, *46* (3), 1195–1221.

Halsted, P. A. "The Conceptual Study of Non-Degree Adult Painting Classes." Unpublished doctoral dissertation, Rutgers University, 1981.

Joyce, M. *First Steps in Teaching Creative Dance: A Handbook for Teachers of Children, Kindergarten Through Sixth Grade.* Palo Alto, Calif.: National Press Books, 1973.

Kaltoft, G. "Music and Emancipatory Learning in Three Community Education Programs." Unpublished doctoral dissertation, Teachers College, 1990.

Knowles, M. S. *The Modern Practice of Adult Education: Andragogy Versus Pedagogy.* New York: Association Press, 1970.

Lerman, L. *Teaching Dance to Senior Adults.* Springfield, Ill.: Thomas, 1984.

Livet, A. (ed.). *Contemporary Dance.* New York: Abbeville Press, 1978.

Louis, M. *Inside Dance.* New York: St. Martin's Press, 1980.

McLeish, J.A.B. *The Ulyssean Adult: Creativity in the Middle and Later Years.* New York: McGraw-Hill, 1976.

Marsick, V. "New Paradigms for Learning in the Workplace." In V. Marsick (ed.), *Learning in the Workplace.* London: Croom-Helm, 1987.

Maslow, A. H. *Toward a Psychology of Being.* (2nd ed.) New York: Van Nostrand Reinhold, 1968.

Rugh, M. M. "The Etiology of Visual Arts Expression with an Older Woman: Patterns of Meaning and Metaphor in Late Life Learning." Unpublished doctoral dissertation, University of Oklahoma, 1990.

Zeph, C. P. "Career Development for Community Adult Educators." *Adult Education Quarterly,* 1991, *41* (3), 217–232.

*ANGELA SGROI is executive assistant to the vice president for academic affairs at Trenton State College in New Jersey. She is an amateur modern dancer by avocation.*

*Understanding the potential for development in older learners can provide educators with insight into a world of meaning through learning.*

# Personal Development Through Learning in Later Life

*Mary Alice Wolf*

> It may even seem that affective, dynamic factors provide the key to all mental development and that in the last analysis it is the need to grow, to assert oneself, to love, and to be admired that constitutes the motive force of intelligence, as well as of behavior in its totality and in its increasing complexity.
> —Jean Piaget (1969, pp. 157–158)

Each older adult learner represents a complex inner world, the result of lifelong stimuli, emotion, and experiences in cognitive and cultural realms. Childhood, early life experience, family "legacies," adult work, love, losses, and renewals connect and reconnect, often in new ways, as we age. Old grievances reemerge, unbidden, into consciousness. Old friends, long gone, touch our daydreams. Memory, deeply personal, resonates with former visions of ourselves, tasks never fully completed, unresolved relationships, abandoned hopes. The future has come: it is the time we have waited for. Yet it is always a surprise, and self-development remains a vibrant possibility. Older adults have the greatest potential for growth and understanding.

We begin to discern these merging notes during the middle years, but we hear the full symphony in old age, the culmination of all human experience. Elders live in the present but can glean meaning from an enriched past and energy through engagement with the future. Older learners are often led into adult education by a quest for self-development and the wish to make meaning of the human experience. This chapter looks at learning from inside that world and attempts to articulate the process of self-development in the older learner. Its goal is to encourage adult educators to explore and appreciate the process of human development in the last stage, the harvest of life. It is based on research and observations of older adults; on data collected through participant observation, diaries, journals, in-depth interviews, and surveys; on information acquired through teaching and writing in the areas of geriatric education, human development, and aging; and on applied work with powerful educational tools: reminiscence and recollection.

## When Does Old Age Begin?

Adulthood is a state of mind. We know that there are stages and rites of passage along the way, but full adulthood involves an awareness of our mortality and the creation of a self that takes command of its attempts to organize experience. Adulthood can be seen as an unloading of the baggage of early life.

The older adult, simply by virtue of time spent in living, is the most complex of all individuals. Old age is indeed an opportunity. Only in older adulthood—that grey area after the passing of middle age—does the human being begin to understand what it means to be "developed." "In old age," says Heschel in Myerhoff's (1979) classic study of elderly Jews, "we got a chance to find out what a human being is, how we could be worthy of being human. You could find in yourself courage, and know you are vital. Then you're living on a different plane. To do this you got to use your brain, but that's not enough. The brain is combined with the soul" (p. 198). In old age, there can be a merging of the knowledge of the body—life's stories—and of the spirit— the developmental potential of the human being. There can be a sense of culmination and competition, what Erikson (1982) calls "integrality."

## Generalizations and Related Educational Implications

Current demographic trends alert us to a great increase in the numbers of older Americans. Life expectancy in the United States has increased dramatically from forty-nine years at the turn of the century to seventy-six years today. Persons over sixty-five constituted less than 5 percent of the U.S. population in 1900; today they make up 12 percent. In the year 2030, the projected population of persons over sixty-five will comprise 21.1 percent of the United States citizenry (United States Bureau of the Census, 1989).

Moody (1988) states that 30 percent of the senior population participates in adult education courses each year. There are one thousand colleges that include elders in classes for credit or audit ("Fast Facts," 1988), and 900,000 persons over the age of sixty-five enrolled in high school or college courses in October of 1986 (United States Senate Special Committee on Aging, 1989). Levels of education differ by cohort (age), region, and race. The older one is, the lower one's educational level is likely to be. For example, 42 percent of persons over seventy-five are high school graduates, compared with 67 percent of persons aged sixty-five (United States Senate Special Committee on Aging, 1989).

Nevertheless, numbers of older learners outwit educators. Elders are the wily fish in the lake who yearly elude the hook. We count them; they frequently populate our adult learning centers and attend Elderhostels. Yet when we prepare our classrooms, older adults may not appear. Curriculum planners scratch their heads, having made elaborate continuing education plans for this elusive "demographic bump." Hiemstra (1985) found that older adults sought learning projects for varied reasons. The majority, however, claimed to learn for "personal enjoyment" and for "self-fulfillment." Surveys, however, can give a distorted view because, though older adults may have similar characteristics, they are often more unalike than at any other time in the life span.

Educational gerontologists thus hesitate to stereotype older persons. As learners, they come ready to penetrate the practitioner's own privately held assumptions about aging. "Will Mr. Smith hear what I'm saying? Is he sleeping or merely listening deeply? Must Mrs. Hendrick *always* disagree with what I'm saying? Is she hostile? Is it true that elders love to reminisce? (This I learned in the research on aging.) Then why does Mrs. Amstead refuse to reminisce? And why has Miss Olger declined to come to class on 'senior evenings' when she is clearly the right age?" As curriculum developers, we cannot always describe our "market."

Nonetheless, by using older learners' stories as testimony or data bases, adult educators *can* reflect on the learning processes in which many older learners engage and can help to plan for them. The following discussion identifies three such processes in ethnographic and survey research that I have conducted over the past fourteen years. These have been gleaned from older learners' discussions of their educational experiences. Though the processes may overlap, I have distinguished them for our observations as follows: learning and meaning-making, learning and the shadow self, and learning and cognitive reordering.

The first process, learning as meaning-making, is found in older learners who may seek enrichment programs such as courses in history, genealogy, philosophy, and ethics. The second, learning and the shadow self, involves the development of skills or characteristics that hitherto have not been part of the older adult's repertoire or represent an early life interest left aside. The third, learning and cognitive reordering, involves an alertness and mindfulness in which the older learner experiences himself or herself in a new and vital way.

## Learning and Meaning-Making

We may find that the deepest of human cravings, the need to find meaning in one's own life experience, often motivates personal learning in old age (Birren and Deutchman, 1991; Erikson, Erikson, and Kivnick, 1986; Hately, 1982; Kaminski, 1984; Moody, 1988; Wolf, 1985 and 1986). Older adults study philosophy, literature, and history as they reflect on their own personal development. A desire for reflection can be a conscious or unconscious agenda in taking adult education courses. Through a seemingly magic process by which the long-term memory takes over and the past comes into focus with astounding clarity, older learners often find new meaning in guided recollection and in reminiscence. They are said to be "settling accounts" through the "universal and normative" process of life review (Butler, 1982).

A Polish refugee now studying history and psychology says, "I want to put together the bits and pieces to make a picture of my life." A seventy-nine-year-old man reminisced in music class: "If you hear a piece of music—it might be a popular piece of music or it might be serious music—your thoughts wander back to the time when you heard it before. Maybe back fifty years. It might put you in the mood that you were in at that time." Paolo, a sixty-nine-year-old retired laborer, found that *all* learning activities stirred memories of his days as a young merchant marine. In a literacy class that dealt with weather, a reminiscence was triggered, and past and present were fused: "Of course, writing about the snow brought back the memories of being up on the bridge when you're steering the ship. And going to Egypt. And there are three stars always together. Three in a row and one on the side. And we use . . . we steer by them stars to get us to our destination. I just got reminded of that out of the blue!"

The process of life review can motivate one to participate in adult education experience, or it can be the natural result of the interactions or content of the class. In a psychology class, Gertrude, age eighty-two, found herself learning about theories of education. She reflected in her journal on the happy days she knew in elementary school and on the fact that she had not continued her education: "I'm not saying that I'm satisfied. You make the best of the situation and accept it. Certainly, I understand now that my parents did all they could for us. And you know, I would have loved nothing better than to have gone on to college and gone on and on and on, but now I just figure, I had to make the best of my life. And that's why I did."

There is a growing literature of curriculum related to reminiscence and the classroom (for example, Kaminsky, 1984; Mulhall and Rowe, 1988; Wolf, 1989). Examples of specific use of this phenomenon are keeping a journal, collecting oral histories, creating drama from early life experiences (Perlstein, 1981; Telander, Quinlan, and Verson, 1982), creating "memory clubs" (Myerhoff, 1979), doing intergenerational biographical projects (Boss, 1990), and writing autobiographically (Birren and Deutchman, 1991; Hately, 1982). Humanities courses, current social policy, psychology curricula, even geography workshops can trigger the reminiscent mode. Although this way of relating to content may motivate many older learners, reminiscence is not *always* operative. As we have learned in adult education planning, if you have met one older adult learner, you have met only one older learner. Do not count on a trend.

## Learning and the Shadow Self

Many older adults are moving into new roles, experimenting with parts of their personalities that were quiescent in earlier life stages. Gutmann (1980), for example, has identified a shifting of gender roles in older adulthood. Women, free of the "parental imperative," may explore the assertive side of their personality. Men, conversely, may now develop their "feminine" selves, their nurturing and creative areas that have been untapped in the structured work world. Jung (1933) described middle age as a turning point in psychic development, a time for exploration of our fuller selves:

> We might compare masculinity and femininity with their psychic components to a particular store of substances of which, in the first half of life, unequal use is made. A man consumes his large supply of masculine substance and has left over only the smaller amount of feminine substance, which he now must put to use. It is the other way around with a woman; she allows her unused supply of masculinity to become active.
>
> This transformation weighs more heavily still in the psychic realm than in the physical. How often it happens that a man of forty or fifty years winds up his business, and that the wife then dons trousers and duties of handyman [pp. 107–108].

While younger generations may not agree with the unliberated images of Jung's gender splitting, we may find examples of growth in older persons who adhered to traditional sex roles. Individuals now in their sixties and seventies belong to a cohort raised to identify "men's work" as out of the home and "women's work" as care taking, feeling, and responding to beauty. Women now may turn to education to train in new careers. Carlotta, age sixty-seven, found herself in a community college setting for the first time in her life. Although she was uncomfortable in the academic milieu, she wanted to study special education: "I want to get the necessary education that I need to go further into this business. So I can know how to deal with the handicapped, you know. Everyone has to be treated different; there are no two alike. I need a learning process that will help me in that field. . . . I'm here for something, and I want to accomplish it." Wuschko, a retired janitor, described the meaning he found in reading literature: "For me it's study for its own sake, or the sake of its beauty. I'm retired now, my most urgent obligations fulfilled. My son finished his education. And now I feel I'm free to indulge myself in certain things I didn't do before."

Personality theorists tell us that we are basically the same throughout our lives (Fiske and Chiriboga, 1990; McCrae and Costa, 1984; Neugarten, 1979). By this, they do not mean to say that we do not change, but, rather, that we grow and develop within a structure that is unique to each of us. Imagine that we are all given a hand of cards at birth, and that throughout life we continue to play these cards, exploring and experimenting with our selfhood. Many older persons are doing just that when they enter the educational world: playing out a card that they have not yet tried. It is the skilled adult educator that sees beyond the sameness of dress style or color of hair in older persons and recognizes, instead, the experimenting and exploring individual coming to class to carry out a personal mandate.

## Learning and Cognitive Reordering

An overlapping paradigm of development involves a cognitive shift that is reflective. Learners are led through a series of activities (both self-directed and serendipitous) because of a wish to experiment, to explore. They are aware of the myths of aging so readily distributed in the media and inculcated in their earlier lives: that older persons are failing and incapable of learning. Yet, sensing themselves in a new way, these learners find that their expectations of older adulthood are not valid; they are *still there,* and vibrantly so. This is a discovery. Each individual feels newly autonomous. Sophie, age seventy, finds her ability startling: "Yes. I think that real learning wakes a person up. I believe that very strongly. The idea is just not to remain static. That is perhaps the most important thing, isn't it? I mean, how does one become a person but to change, to keep risking, trying out new ways of looking at things?"

Madeline H., seventy-four-years-old, wrote the following in an adult education class:

> Was I once a fish
> long and flat and round of eye?
> White-fine bone in classic structure,
> Glistening scale in primal pattern,
> Gliding through the silent seasons,
> Soundless, mindless,
> Knowing only fish fulfillment—
> Was I?

The poem, she says, represents her personal growth in the ten years since she began her education. Her current life is confining, as she cares for an ill husband and seldom goes out. Her primary "selfish" experience is her weekly adult education class. Without it, she says, she would return to the stagnant world of the fish, her former self. She writes:

> Life
> Leave it? Never!
> Taller than chimneys, lighter than smoke,
> Warm as the sun, fair as the sounds
> of spring, Being
> shall occupy all.
>
> Rising complete with loosened loveliness
> that melts all imperfect bonds
> the spirit shall turn to
> Immortal form.

Madeline represents the seeker of learning whose process is deeply personal and who is enriched by interacting with a world of spirit. She comes to class to expand this development and is nourished through interaction with peers and teachers. The opportunity for self-expression is essential to her well-being at this time in her life.

There is also pleasure in play during the last part of life. The concept is not new to theorists and researchers who have observed elders engaged in games such as bingo. Indeed, Piaget (1962) found a direct relationship between cognitive development and play, stressing the vast array of inventions by which the individual understands and assimilates to the environment. The elder, with a developmental mandate to achieve wisdom, may need to experiment and relive the inventive phases of childhood exploration and cognitive reordering. Stone (1989) defines *play* as follows: "I consider play to be *any* activity undertaken for its own sake. . . . Only humans undertake actions simply because they are choice-worthy, and these actions constitute what is most noble in human affairs" (pp. 64-65). There is an ongoing need to play, of which Erikson observed, "We regard lifelong expressions of playfulness, throughout the work ethos as well as in recreation and creativity" (Erikson, Erikson, and Kivnick, 1986, p. 169).

In this third form of learning (cognitive reordering), the individual may wish to be connected to others. There may be a restlessness, a need to touch and be part of the world. It is a fear of human loss, of impoverishment. We can say, "I am awake; I am here." There is pleasure of survivorship and a continued investment in living.

This category is marked by awareness or attention to the experience. Learning is the extension of the process, a zestful realization of the self. Cognitive reordering involves a creative tension, a wish to be more fully alive. As Csikszentmihalyi (1990) says, "Attention is our most important tool in the task of improving the quality of experience" (p. 33). The learner involved in this process is curious about a wide variety of content and seeks a heightened interaction with the environment. Theorists describe this cognitive level as wisdom, crystallized intelligence: "It appears desirable to focus on the basic notion of crystallized intelligence as a 'developmentally higher-level' factor covering culturally influenced, individually acquired and maintained abilities for understanding and thinking" (Dittmann-Kohli and Baltes, 1990, p. 58).

The three processes observed here, learning and meaning-making, learning and the shadow self, and learning and cognitive reordering, are not unique to older adults. They are the means by which we all sometimes come to terms with our experience at transitional times in our lives, times of awakened consciousness and search for self-development. There is a need to be engaged; we feel challenged to grow. Older learners, however, are often particularly purposeful in seeking the missing pieces of their histories. Time, they now know, is precious. "I do not have forever, you know," says Greta, age eighty-one. "What I spend my time on has to count." Although many older persons are active, energy levels do limit choices. "There are only so many hours in the day," states James M., "and I like to line them up right." "If I'm ever going to learn to use a computer," asks Sister Mildred, age seventy-two, "what better time?"

The three categories discussed here encompass a wide range of potential routes to self-development. They may operate easily and in tandem or they may be combined in a burst of self-discovery and abandon. Each of us has that metaphorical hand of cards and a unique personality that dictate how we play out our game. When the environment is friendly, we will grow through exploration in these three modes.

## Role of the Teacher

How does the adult educator respond with a greater understanding of the older learner? First, by clearing the learning environment of stereotypical and belittling factors; second, by achieving a greater appreciation of all human development—including his or her own; third, by exploring the processes by which learners achieve integrity and joy; fourth, by adopting curricula and experiences that enhance the learning potential of older adults.

Working with the older learner is a reciprocal process; warmth is often the key to interchange. The learner requires the teacher to be genuine, authentic. "Learned" models of pedagogy or andragogy will not replace the actual comfort level that can be reached when the teacher is genuine.

## Conclusions, Cautions, and Phenomenology

**Allow Older People to Identify Themselves as Individuals.** They are not sentimental objects and should not be mythologized. Often educators stamp the older person as "quaint." Growing older does not alter one's lifelong persona: one is not suddenly wise or frail. Hilda M., age seventy-two, stated: "I will confess to you—I'm old. But it's nothing like what you see on the outside. You see an old lady, and you think she's thinking this and that. I'm the same me inside, and I know what it's like to be eighteen and to be forty. I'm going all the time inside, and I want to keep on going. I thought I'd be all finished with some of this thinking about myself by this age, but I'm not. I'm certainly not." Create an environment where each older person can determine his or her persona, based on inner self-image and not on assumptions arising from physical appearance.

**Create Morale-Building Environments.** Let us reeducate the scores of older adults who would diminish their own lives by hiding behind outdated stereotypes. And let us find ways to incorporate freedom of growth and development rather than decline into our schoolwide curricula. Many older people fear the loss of cognitive abilities. They equate school with tests and judgmental instructors and often feel threatened by the perceived loss of intellectual ability. Educators would do well to introduce recollective discussions into the classroom. Here, older learners' experiences with such subjects as business cycles, wars, and weather can provide vivid background information. With growing numbers of better-educated older persons entering classrooms in future years, we will need to revise curricula further.

**Listen to the Intrapsychic Voices of Older Adults.** The responsive adult educator will touch the lives of learners if she or he appreciates the worlds of older persons. The educator might adopt the attitude that older persons cannot be stereotyped, that they hold several cards yet in their hands, and that a risk-free environment will encourage playing these out.

Trust is the building block for all human interactions; trust between the learner and the educator is built on mutual respect. Education has the greatest potential for the older person. When the context is rich and supportive, older persons have the greatest work to do. They have the developmental mandate to make sense of life, to leave a legacy of meaning and trust to coming generations, and to say that their lives have meant and continue to mean something. They want to be fully alive. What finer role can education play?

**Consider Developing Outreach Activities for Institutionalized Elders.** Their attention span, locus of control, and selfhood can be revived through stimulating experiences. We must shift our perceptions of how to nourish physically frail elders. A volunteer in a nursing home wrote the following about her Monday morning group:

> I have been continuing to offer my workshop now titled "Humanities," to a group of seniors at the Hebrew Home. I started with five and we now usually have anywhere from fifteen to twenty people. What a joy it is to share readings with these people! I have witnessed a genuine flowering

of their personalities. Many were very shy and withdrawn and now they are not only verbal but show their feelings of sadness or laughter.

But what is most amazing to me is how mentally sharp they are and what wisdom they have to share. We have covered so many topics from "Zen and the Art of Seeing" to Haiku poetry to going "On the Road with Charles Kuralt." Now they are bringing in poetry they have written to share with the group and reminiscing with their own stories from the past.

I experimented by bringing a dementia patient into the group one week. She hummed her way down the halls and I thought her humming to herself might be a problem while I was reading. I asked another volunteer to stay for a while in the group just in case this resident wouldn't be quiet. To my surprise, not only was she silent during the readings, but she listened intently and responded at appropriate times with the appropriate emotions. It occurred to me that it is possible to offer programs like this to dementia patients in beginning stages of the disease.

When I first came to the group I was very aware of their infirmities. Now I see them much more as people than as patients [Atkins, 1991].

Finally, we have to admit that none of us truly understands aging. This is built into our cultural ethos. It is also true that we wish to stay the same; we wish for those around us to remain in place. Educators would do well to extend their own understanding of development. We would do well to appreciate that life is a continual process of change from the moment of our conception to the moment of our death. Each of us, if we are lucky, will live a long and full life. (The alternative, Woody Allen reminds us, is not at all attractive.) Each of us must age, and each of us must die. It is what we *do* with our days that matters. In this, elders are no different from anyone else. Indeed, there is no "them" and "us." Perhaps the understanding of aging and the older adult learner is simply the understanding of all human beings who seek to grow to their fullest potential, and the learning that older persons engage in is the expression of this phenomenon.

## References

Atkins, B. K. "Human Development II Journal." Unpublished journal for Human Development II class, Saint Joseph College, West Hartford, Conn., 1991.

Birren, J. E., and Deutchman, D. *Guiding Autobiography Groups for Older Adults.* Baltimore: Johns Hopkins University Press, 1991.

Boss, J. *The Benefits of Intergenerational Reminiscence for Three Diverse Groups.* Paper presented at the annual meeting of the Northeastern Gerontological Society, New Haven, Conn., Apr. 20, 1990.

Butler, R. N. "Successful Aging and the Role of the Life Review." In S. H. Zarit (ed.), *Readings in Aging and Death: Contemporary Perspectives.* New York: HarperCollins, 1982.

Csikszentmihalyi, M. *Flow: The Psychology of Optimal Experience.* New York: HarperCollins, 1990.

Dittmann-Kohli, R., and Baltes, P. B. "Toward a Neofunctionalist Conception of Adult Intellectual Development: Wisdom as a Prototypical Case of Intellectual Growth." In C. N. Alexander and E. J. Langer (eds.), *Higher Stages of Human Development.* New York: Oxford University Press, 1990.

Erikson, E. *The Life Cycle Completed.* New York: Norton, 1982.

Erikson, E., Erikson, J., and Kivnick, H. Q. *Vital Involvement in Old Age.* New York: Norton, 1986.

"Fast Facts." *Mature Market Report,* 1988, 5 (May).

Fiske, M., and Chiriboga, D. A. *Change and Continuity in Adult Life.* San Francisco: Jossey-Bass, 1990.

Gutmann, D. L. "An Exploration of Ego Configurations in Middle and Later Life." In B. L. Neugarten and others (L. Stein, ed.), *Personality in Middle and Late Life.* New York: Arno Press, 1980.

Hately, B. J. "Guided Autobiography: An Approach to Human Development." Paper presented at the 35th annual scientific meeting of the Gerontological Society of America, Boston, Nov. 22, 1982.

Hiemstra, R. "The Older Adult's Learning Projects." In D. B. Lumsden (ed.), *The Older Adult as Learner.* New York: Hemisphere Publishing, 1985.

Jung, C. G. *Modern Man in Search of a Soul.* (W. S. Dell and C. F. Baynes, trans.) Orlando, Fla.: Harcourt Brace Jovanovich, 1933.

Kaminsky, M. (ed.). *The Uses of Reminiscence: New Ways of Working with Older Adults.* New York: Dutton, 1984.

McCrae, R., and Costa, P. T. *Emerging Lives, Enduring Dispositions: Personality in Adulthood.* Boston: Little, Brown, 1984.

Moody, G. R. "Introduction." *Generations,* 1987-88, 12 (2), 5-9.

Moody, G. R. *Abundance of Life.* New York: Columbia University Press, 1988.

Mulhall, D., and Rowe, K. *A Time For . . . A Six-Session, Small-Group Discussion Process with Older Adults.* Los Angeles: Franciscan Communications, 1988.

Myerhoff, B. *Number Our Days.* New York: Dutton, 1979.

Neugarten, B. L. "Personality and the Aging Process." In S. H. Zarit (ed.), *Readings in Aging and Death: Contemporary Perspectives.* New York: HarperCollins, 1979.

Perlstein, S. *A Stage for Memory.* New York: Teachers and Writers Collaborative Publications, 1981.

Piaget, J. *Play, Dreams, and Imitation in Childhood.* (C. Gattegno and F. M. Hodgson, trans.) New York: Norton, 1962.

Piaget, J., and Inhelder, B. *The Psychology of the Child.* (H. Weaver, trans.) New York: Basic Books, 1969.

Stone, B. L. "The Self and the Play-Element in Culture." *Play and Culture,* 1989, 2, 64-79.

Telander, M., Quinlan, F., and Verson, K. *Acting Up!* Chicago: Coach House Press, 1982.

United States Bureau of the Census. *Statistical Abstract.* Washington, D.C.: U.S. Government Printing Office, 1989.

United States Senate Special Committee on Aging. *Aging America.* Washington, D.C.: U.S. Government Printing Office, 1989.

Wolf, M. A. "The Experience of Older Learners in Adult Education." *Lifelong Learning,* 1985, 8 (5), 8-11.

Wolf, M. A. "Backwards and Forwards: An Approach to Understanding the Older Learner." Paper presented to the annual meeting of the American Association for Adult and Continuing Education, Hollywood, Fla., 1986.

Wolf, M. A. "Reminiscence: A Gift from the Aged." In E. A. Secord (ed.), *Ministry with and for Older Adults.* New Haven, Conn.: Office of Urban Affairs for the Archdiocese of Hartford, 1989.

*MARY ALICE WOLF is director of the Institute in Gerontology and associate professor of human development/gerontology at Saint Joseph College, West Hartford, Connecticut.*

*Study circles, in one form or another, have been with us since our founding. Now that they have been reintroduced to further collaborative adult learning in America, it is time to consider how the individual adult learner grows from the study circle experience.*

# Study Circles: Individual Growth Through Collaborative Learning

*Leonard P. Oliver*

We can learn and act as individuals, in groups, or in larger societal contexts—whatever the social or political system. Study circles, however, can only thrive in a democratic atmosphere, since one of the abiding tenants of a study circle, wherever it is found, is voluntary and equal democratic participation. Every study circle member has an equal voice; everyone "sits in the front row." This practice means that participants determine the agenda and outcomes, or public judgments (as the Kettering Foundation's National Issues Forums likes to call them). The results cannot be preconceived, as in most adult education programs that are teacher or authority-driven. Unpredictability and uncertainty of outcomes are the antithesis of authoritarian control.

Study circles practice the art of citizenship, teaching individuals to function democratically. For the Swedes, who perfected the modern study circle format from its introduction in the late 1800s, they are miniature democracies—a way to make civil society, as well as complex organizations, work democratically.

Study circles encourage collaborative learning in small groups through participant-led, sequential sessions. The learning that takes place in study circles, both from the content and the process, is then carried over to individual and collective decision making—in the work place, in community life, and in political affairs.

Learning in study circles is not new. From Ben Franklin's Junto, to Josiah Holbrook's Lyceums and their lecture-teaching-community study circles, to Reverend John Vincent's Chautauqua Literacy and Scientific

Circle's 15,000 home study circles at the turn of the century, Americans have sought company in their opinions. The study circle is rooted in John Adams's notion that Americans could only realize freedom if they were educated and responsible civic citizens. Popular sovereignty implies an informed and participating population. According to Christopher Lasch (1991): "What democracy requires is public debate, not information. . . . When we get into arguments that focus and fully engage our attention, we become avid seekers of relevant information. Otherwise, we take information passively—if we take it in at all" (p. 72).

Throughout our history, study circles or some form of small-group discussion have been a cornerstone of adult education, particularly adult civic education. By the early 1900s, the idea made its way to Sweden, where the study circle became integral to the development of the new social movements: trade unions, the temperance movement, the free church, the Social Democratic Party, cooperatives, and the YMCAs and YWCAs. The "popular movements," as they are called in Sweden, used the study circle as a natural vehicle for adult education, creating educational opportunities for adults who had limited formal education. The study circles taught members about their organizations and about democratic participation in an organization or community; in the process, they uncovered new leadership from circle members. What was learned in the study circle subsequently carried over into political life, as most of the popular movements eventually became active in political affairs (Oliver, 1987).

The late Swedish Prime Minister, Olof Palme, once called Sweden "a study circle democracy" (Workers' Educational Association, 1973, p. 1). Indeed, with 320,000 study circles every year attracting 2.9 million adults to collaborative small-group learning, with over $100 million in annual subsidies for the circles, and with sixty thousand paid study circle organizers—study circles constitute the bulk of what is known as the Swedish "learning society," accompanied by the folk high schools and the municipal adult education courses.

Henry Blid (1989) provides a splendid history of the Swedish study circles, and the newly formed Study Circles Resource Center (SCRC) offers a range of materials, both domestic and international, on study circle history, philosophy, pedagogy, and practice. As the modern study circle has certain defined characteristics and guiding principles, mostly derived from the Swedish experience, let us examine these principles before we assess the kind of individual learning that can take place in the study circle context. The principles are an amalgam derived from the work of Oliver (1987), Blid (1990), and the SCRC (1990). They are important because they underlie all study circle work, permit consistency of format in diverse settings, and form the basis for individual growth through collaborative learning—the subject of this chapter.

*Convenient, Inexpensive, and Informal Adult Learning Setting.* Ideally, a study circle has a minimum of five and a maximum of twenty participants, including the leader, so it can meet in any convenient small-group setting. The only costs are materials (which may be free), recruitment materials, and refreshments. Study circles need no formal institutional support, no exams, no content experts, no prerequisites, and no required texts. They provide pure and simple adult learning. All study circles meet more than once to enable participants to come to know each other's views, reflect on the learning, reinforce the learning by application, and prepare for the next session.

*Well-Prepared Leader.* The study circle leader is well prepared—through formal training, experience in small-group settings, or exposure to written/ video training materials. The leader is neither teacher nor content expert, does not set the agenda, but does maintain balance and encourages full participation.

*Print, Video, and Audio Materials as Catalysts for Discussion.* Study circle materials—print, video, audio—serve to stimulate discussion, frame the issue for the participants, provide a logical sequence for the discussions, and bring out the collective experience of the participants. They are not self-standing texts; they are only useful when used as catalysts to elicit participants' views and values.

*Democratic Atmosphere with Equality of Participation.* Every participant has an equal opportunity to speak in the study circle, every opinion carries weight, and no person or persons should dominate a study circle. Participants are recognized as equals, all opinions are sought out, and participants are expected to listen to differing views.

*Adult Education Learning Principles in Every Study Circle.* Because study circles are voluntary learning settings, adults come with a readiness to learn and with experiences to enrich the discussions. This situation means that no two study circles are alike; despite the similarity of materials, the participants' experiences, once brought out, make each study circle unique. Study circle knowledge should be practical, fitting into the adult's need for usable knowledge, and capable of being applied to problem situations. Finally, the goal of all study circles, like the goal of adult education, is self-directed learning.

*Collaborative Learning for Change, Growth, and Action.* Study circle learning is collaborative, not competitive, with participants learning from the process of cooperation as well as from the content. This emphasis is especially important when discussing social and political issues, as such knowledge is public and shared, not individual. By sharing knowledge, by tolerating differing perspectives, participants learn how to function together in a community and to find values in common that enable them to strive for change and collective action.

These principles apply whether the study circle operates under the auspices of the National Issues Forums (NIF), the International Union of

Bricklayers and Allied Craftsmen (BAC), the Public Talk Series sponsored by the Study Circle Resource Center (SRC), or one of the hundreds of organizations throughout the country currently using study circles for both member and community education. Substantial study circle activity in America is a recent phenomenon, given a boost by the NIF, SRC, and, surprisingly, the *Utne Reader* (1991), which devoted an issue to several variations of study circles.

Study circles in America are now under way on national health care reform (AFL-CIO), the role of America in the world (NIF), national economic policy (SCRC), union organizing (BAC), and dozens of other important issues. Organizations are using study circles to inform their members, to examine their futures, and to relate to community issues. The Gulf War triggered a media outcry for public debate, but we have few mechanisms in America to involve the public on such short notice and in such a direct way. One congressman, Sam Gejdenson (D-Conn.), discovered study circles and promoted discussion about the Gulf War in his congressional district, using the study circle format. He had such a promising response that he is working with the SCRC to take on other pressing issues.

## The Dynamics of Collaborative Learning Through Study Circles

More and more, study circles are being employed for the discussion of social and political issues, both within organizations and in the community. This form of collaborative learning is not new. Americans have always felt the need in difficult times to come together to resolve pervasive social and political issues—or, as the Kettering Foundation calls them in *Hard Choices,* "value-laden issues" (1991). Collaborative learning in this sense is a counter to individualized, often competitive learning situations for adults; the common theme, as the Kettering Foundation puts it, is that "in a democracy, the people must decide on the nature of the common public interests. In order to do that, they must make difficult choices on a wide array of issues" (p. 5). The foundation calls this "choice work," and it holds whether the study circle is found within an organization wrestling with its future or within a community struggling with weighty public policy decisions.

Both organizations and communities have used small-discussion groups to address these issues, but what is new in the current climate is the widespread adoption and acceptance of the term *study circle,* encouraging consistency in format and comparisons across diverse organizations and communities.

Study circles occur in different settings, across socio-economic-political spectrums, and with such varied participants as adult literacy students, construction workers, retirees, organizational activists, and middle- and upper-middle-class community residents interested in the idea of collaborative learning. Here are a few of the settings in which study circles have flourished in the United States.

**The Organizational Study Circle.** The following are examples of organizations that had a need to bring participants together in an educational setting. An organizational study circle would tend to promote the organization's agenda, leaving it to the study circle participants to enrich the range of choices available for decision making.

1. *International Union of Bricklayers and Allied Craftsmen.* Workers in construction trades tend to work from job to job, often having no fixed plant/factory site. In this situation, the BAC found it difficult to develop a member education program. Armed with a recent report from its Project 2000 Committee, charged with developing alternatives for the union's future, BAC leaders decided in 1986 to launch a pilot study circle program to obtain members' views on the future of the union. The results were dramatic, with 88 percent of the participants recommending continuation of the program, 89 percent stating that they had an equal opportunity in the give-and-take discussions, 63 percent saying that they identified more strongly with the union future plans, and a sizable majority reporting that they felt greater confidence in working on union affairs and solving their own problems. BAC subsequently trained over two hundred local study circle leaders and has developed new study circle curricula on union-organizing and health care issues.

2. *Health Care Education Associates.* Under a grant from the National Institute on Aging, Rita Strombeck, president of Health Care Education Associates, devised a four-session study circle for preretirees and retirees on national health care issues and reform of America's health and long-term care system. The materials, designed to trigger discussion about this vital topic, include case studies, additional readings, and discussion questions for the participants. The leader's guide takes the leader through each session with sample questions, ideas related to group dynamics, session questionnaires, and ideas for community action after the study circle ends. Strombeck believes that the study circle format will be effective in communicating to the participants that they are not alone in their apprehensions about retiree health care and will enrich the learning through the interactive process.

3. *New York State Education Department's "Action Education" Program.* The New York State Education Department's Bureau of Home Economics and Technology Education Programs initiated its Action Education study circle program in May 1990 to build leadership skills in Future Homemakers of America chapters across the state. Marilyn H. Klink, program coordinator, believes that the study circle offers an ideal format for leadership development, as leadership skills "begin with the individual but ripple outward." The department's study circles are designed to provide a means for students to develop and practice leadership skills in the small-group

setting, eventually building leadership teams. The program developed a comprehensive guide that introduces study circles, presents strategies for building group cohesion and leadership, and includes ideas for planning and evaluation (New York State Education Department, 1990).

**The Community-Based Study Circle.** Community study circles, developed for the discussion of public issues, would more likely employ the concept of choice work. These might present a spectrum of value-based choices in the discussion materials and encourage participants to work through the choices. The goals of these study circles are more informed citizens and outcomes that could result in collective citizen action.

1. *National Issues Forums Study Circles.* More than 1,300 communities across the country engage in public issue discussion on three major topics of national concern every fall, with approximately one-half of these programs using the study circle format. Other formats include the larger public forum, combined forums and study circles, and at times the addition of local media—primarily television and newspapers. The study circles use the NIF issue booklets distributed in the late summer every year as catalysts for discussion, accompanied by video and audiotapes. Leaders (NIF conveners and moderators) are trained in Summer Public Policy Institutes held regionally. Study circle participants work through the issues with their friends and neighbors, confronting the difficult choices we all face on such issues as remedies for racial inequality, regaining America's competitive edge, and the battle over abortion—the 1990 issues. The 1991 issues are energy policy for the 1990s, income inequality, and America's role in the world. The NIF is designed to give the public a voice in policy deliberations, and it encourages new community and political relationships: "They discovered the power to put people together in different ways, and so to begin changing the political environment of the community" (Kettering Foundation, 1991, p. 35).

2. *Study Circle Resource Center's Public Talk Series.* The Gulf Crisis inspired an outpouring of sentiments by columnists and politicians alike for more public debate. Public hearings, town meetings, informal community discussions—all started to address the issue, with Congress listening intently. In the month before President Bush's deadline to the Iraqis, the SCRC put out its booklet, *Crisis in the Gulf,* which touched a public nerve; there were 3,200 inquiries about the booklet and the SCRC. The SCRC decided to name its program the Public Talk Series and began framing other issues on the congressional and public agenda: America's role in the Middle East, American society and economic policy, cultural diversity, and the death penalty. The booklets describe the choices for each issue in eight to ten pages and include discussion questions, suggestions for both study circle leaders and participants, and follow-up reporting forms. Plans are under way to share the results of the Public Talk Series with policy makers. It is too early to determine the effectiveness of the Public Talk Series

approach, but by taking on immediate contemporary issues being discussed in legislative halls, the SCRC may have struck on a formula to excite both community study circle participants and their elected representatives who want more than public opinion polls and mass town meetings.

3. *National Issue Forums Literacy Program for Correctional Institutions.* The NIF's issue books are written for regular readers and in an abridged edition for adult literacy students. Almost all the NIF literacy programs are study circles, convenient to the institutions and communities sponsoring NIF. The NIF Corrections Program reaches into prisons to involve inmates in the study circle discussions. The program encourages inmates to discuss national public issues, bringing them into the policy deliberations and making them part of the larger society, through the balloting that takes place after the sessions. At the Clallam Bay Corrections Center in Washington State, for example, inmates read the issue book, discuss it, and write essays about it. One Clallam instructor said: "Regardless of their literacy level, the students are able to enter into the discussions because the issues are relevant to their lives." At the Westville Correctional Center in Indiana, inmates' study circles on drugs, crime, and the environment have been reported in local papers, and the center has made videos of the circles in action. The NIF is used to change inmate attitudes about society and themselves and to improve their communications skills. Citizenship is enhanced, the center's staff talk about the inmates' greater self-esteem, increased sense of belonging to society, and head start on leaving prison. Inmate participation is voluntary, and a centerwide forum caps the annual round of study circles.

## Study Circles: Faith in the Democratic Process

The examples offered in preceding paragraphs demonstrate the power of the study circle to bring individuals to adult learning—be they construction workers, prison inmates, retirees, home economics students, or the average citizen. The fact that these people have sought out the study circle experience puts to rest some of the myths and stereotypes about adult learning: that construction workers do not want to read, that prison inmates are not interested in issues like day care and education, that retirees are more concerned with how to grow old than discussing national issues, and that the average citizen is apathetic on public issues, preferring sitcoms to civic learning. One of the reasons these stereotypes have been perpetuated, at times even influencing the way situations and organizations relate to their members and constituents, is the absence of adult education mechanisms that emphasize the individual's views and need to be recognized. Citizens avoid mass meetings because their views are lost in the shuffle. Rank-and-file union members are notorious for avoiding union business meetings because the agendas are preset by the leadership.

Inmates avoid typical classroom instruction because this is where they struck out in the first place.

Collaborative learning, through study circles, changes the usual teacher/professional role of the expert dispensing knowledge to passive adult students. The study circle leader is not an authority figure, but a guide to help adult learners to work together, to analyze problems jointly, to come up with common actions. In contrast to the typical classroom situation or workshop where subject matter flows from the teachers/panelists/ content experts to the adult students, both leaders and participants have knowledge to be shared, and the study circle with its democratic format encourages this exchange.

Collaborative learning is all the more important when participants are expected to take part in the decision-making process. If organizational members, employee citizens, or institutional constituents are expected to influence policy making, then they need the types of information available to decision makers to enable them to participate on an equal basis. One result of the study circle process, therefore, is to change the way adult students view education. If we expect adults to participate democratically in their organizations and communities, why should we not expect them to participate democratically in the educational process that enables them to take part? Why do we leave democracy at the doorstep of adult learning? Should not adult education be about stimulating the adult learners to make decisions for themselves and to act on the type of informed public judg-ments that arise from the free and open discussion of equals? The alterna-tive is continued dependence on authority, on experts, on the media, on everyone but ourselves. If one of our goals in adult education is to encour-age adults to understand and to think critically and act responsibly about our public judgments, the process should be deliberative, democratic, and participatory to promote these behaviors.

## The Adult Learner in the Study Circle Context

Are individuals really different as a result of participating in a study circle experience? Have they grown through the collaborative learning process? What evidence beyond the anecdotal can we find to ascertain just what happens to an individual in the study circle? Even though we have yet to document the study circle experience beyond the anecdotal and the several Swedish studies mentioned above, perhaps we can place the study circle in the context of small-group discussions generally.

From the Swedish experience with the study circles over the course of this century, we can safely say that study circles are synonymous with adult education in Sweden; or, as one Swedish trade unionist told me, "I can't imagine our union or our Social Democratic Party without study circles." We also know from the Swedish experience, and from our own experiences with the NIF and the Bricklayers' Union, that study circles uncover and develop new leadership, that individuals come to understand a collective way of thinking about issues and decision making, and that participants can gain a sense of capacity and power to affect organizations and public life. We also have some evidence, particularly from the NIF Literacy Program, that study circles can move individuals from dependence on authority figures to independent, self-directed learning (Hurley, 1991). So let us look at some work that relates to, but is not directly associated with, the study circle phenomenon.

## The Study Circle as a Small-Group Phenomenon

Research on the efficiency of small-group discussion versus lecture-type, information-dispensing adult education formats goes back to the social-psychologist, Kurt Lewin. Using small-group discussion, he worked with housewives during World War II to encourage the eating of organ meats and produced research influencing adult education for several decades thereafter. "Group dynamics" introduced the group way of learning, created new terminologies and techniques (role playing, feedback, buzz groups), and advocated training adults to participate in society. Discussion became the basic method of adult education—strengthening the discussion and group-work method strengthens democracy.

Much of the work on small-group discussion over the years has focused on the classroom setting and has been known variously as cooperative or collaborative learning, experiential small-group learning, and discussion as a learning strategy. Most of the findings show the small-group technique to be effective when the group has time to work through issues and allow everyone to participate, but it is less efficient when there is a substantial body of material to cover in a limited time frame. Also, the small-group methodology works well in the classrooms with dependent learners, but less well with highly independent learners. The researchers talk about small groups instilling democratic values, encouraging participation, stimulating interest, and enriching students' own sense of expertise (Sharan, 1989–1990; Kuriloff, 1988; Boston, 1989; Friedmann, 1989; and Crowley, 1989).

## The Study Circle: Experiential Education in Action

If, as some writers argue, knowledge is inherently social in nature, then a pedagogical style that emphasizes cooperative efforts among learners and common inquiry can be highly effective (Sheridan, 1989). Cooperative learning implies getting to know other participants, their backgrounds, their views on the issues, and, most importantly, their value systems. Study circle leaders emphasize setting this information out early, putting each person's ideas on the table, so that everyone participates in some way in the first session—essentially the "first speech" that makes all subsequent deliberation easier.

In training study circle leaders, we often refer to Kolb's experiential learning model (1981). Applied to adult education, the experiential learning model creates a base of valuable information about the participants that an effective leader can build upon. In mass meetings, in most classrooms, in our full-agenda, fast-paced world, individual experiences can often be over-looked, we never come to know each other, and the dialogue suffers.

Kolb (1981) places emphasis upon the match-up between "personal learning styles" and the "learning demands of different and unique disciplines" (p. 235). His experiential learning model consists of four steps:

1. Concrete experience
2. Observations and reflections
3. Formation of abstract concepts and generalization
4. Testing implications of concepts in new situations.

Study circles seem most effective when dealing with social-political, economic-cultural issues, not subjects that require individual mastery of complex principles and masses of data. Following Kolb's schema, effective study circles should start with participants' immediate, concrete experiences. These form the basis for participant observation and reflection, using the personal insights, study circle discussion, and interaction with the leader and other participants to build an idea, seek commonalities with others, and begin the process of seeking explanations for the experiences: learning by doing.

The next step in the model, formulating abstract concepts and generalizations, enables the participants to identify their experiences with an issue conceptually, to understand the issue abstractly, and to relate it to the printed materials. The final step, application of the learning, simply implies coming to grips with the issue, looking at alternatives, and creating a basis for actions that lead to new concrete experiences.

Once exposed to experiential learning, following Kolb's model, most adults will find it difficult to enter another learning situation where their experiences are discounted or where the teacher dominates. What the study circle teaches is that individuals are important—their stories, their experiences, their values, their opinions. Adult education can only benefit. The community and the society will also benefit.

## Study Circles: Building Capacity for Participation

Vestland's study (1981) is one of the few research projects to document the effect of study circles on the community, but Swedish literature has touted the capacitating power of study circles almost since their introduction to Sweden ninety years ago.

We know that knowledge is the key to power; that democratic participation in public life is infectious; that study circles can aid citizens in being able to reflect on and analyze issues; and that, if views and judgments are taken seriously in the study circle setting, then people expect them to be taken seriously in their organizations and communities. Study circle leaders and participants are learning the skills of listening creatively, developing ideas and presenting them to a group, and discussing and working together to find common ground on which to build collective action. The result can be increased self-confidence, organizational and community unity, and new voices, ideas, and relationships in organizational and community decision making. The Swedes found this out in linking the study circle to their popular movements; now we are rediscovering the capacity-building value of the modern study circle, where every individual's voice is heard, where people see wisdom and power in collective action.

## The Leadership-Enhancing Role of the Study Circle

Closely related to the notion of building individual capacity for action and decision making through study circles is leadership development. The Swedes admit that many of the leaders in their popular movements—the trade unions, the environmental groups, the political parties, the cooperatives—only became visible after surfacing in the study circle discussions.

The study circle leader, usually as a result of study circle training and experience with small groups, understands the need for fairness, for reconciliation, for respect for the concerns and values of study circle members, for reflection on the characteristics and needs of individual members, and for movement toward the participants' goals. Any leader, in any walk of life, will easily recognize the necessity of these attributes. Just as they are critical to a successful study circle, they are equally essential to the conduct of leadership in organizational and public life. After all, leadership connotes problem solving. Study circles help to make complex problems seem manageable by reducing them to their simplest components, by tracing them to their origins, by bringing in individual values to shed light on each aspect, and by showing that solutions to more tractable problems can provide answers to larger, more complex ones. This process can only take place in the give-and-take of a democratic small group. It can only take place with skilled leadership.

The new era of leadership requires new processing for the communication of ideas, for education—be it civic, employee, or organizational. Study circles seem to be emerging at a propitious time. Leadership is not created by the experience of being told what to learn and how to learn it. Leaders and their enlightened followers can only come from democratic participation that enables individuals to challenge and to choose among the values that order and guide their lives, to think critically, to take responsibility for organizational and civic life, and to connect with others. Study circles have the potential to instill and develop these qualities.

When I think about the individual growth that can come from collaborative learning in formats like the study circle, I think about what it means to say that "everyone can sit in the front row"; I also think about Myles Horton's eloquent statement about why he founded the Highlander Folk School in the early 1930s (Woodside, 1990):

> I'd like to see people develop their own resources, and I'd like to help them do it, not do it for them. . . . If we really wanted to help people, we'd let them help themselves learn to be self-sustaining instead of dependent. . . . We need more democracy. . . . Everybody has their own definition of democracy, and I have mine. Mine is complete democracy, in every walk of life—in the homes, in the factory, in the community, in the state. . . . I believe we ought to do things in groups. People need the stimulation of the group. They also need the strength of the group, and they need to get ideas from other people in the group who have situations similar to theirs. Ideas that are useful can grow out of that sort of discussion. You have to stand up for what you believe in, but you can't do it without the support of the people [pp. 22-23].

Horton could easily have been describing study circles. By sharing in our learning as adults, we are sharing our ability to grow, change ourselves, and improve our society. The Swedes discovered this simple truth as their nation entered the twentieth century. It is our turn to discover it as we enter the twenty-first century.

## References

Blid, H. *Education by the People—Study Circles.* Ludvika, Sweden: Brunsvik Folk High School, 1989.

Blid, H. "Adult Learning in Study Circles." Paper presented at the Brunsvik Folk High School, Ludvika, Sweden, 1990.

Boston, J. "Teaching/Learning Collaboratively." *Social Studies Review,* 1989, *28* (3), 3-6.

Crowley, P. M. "Ask the Expert: A Group Teaching Tool." *Journal for Specialists in Group Work,* 1989, *14* (3), 173-175.

Friedmann, M. "Stimulating Classroom Learning with Small Groups." *Music Educators Journal,* 1989, *76* (2), 53-56.

Hurley, M. E. "Empowering Adult Learners." *Adult Learning,* 1991, 2 (4), 20-23, 27.

Kettering Foundation. *Hard Choices: An Introduction to the National Issues Forums.* Dayton, Ohio: Kettering Foundation, 1991.

Kolb, D. A. "Learning Styles and Disciplinary Differences." In A. W. Chickering (ed.), *The Modern American College: Responding to the New Realities of Diverse Students and a Changing Society.* San Francisco: Jossey-Bass, 1981.

Kuriloff, P. J. "Mechanisms That Contribute to Learning in Experiential Small Groups." *Small Group Behavior*, 1988, *19* (2), 207–226.

Lasch, C. "The Art of Political Argument." *Utne Reader*, 1991, *44*, 72–73.

New York State Education Department. *Action Education: Using Study Circles to Build Student Leadership Teams.* New York: State Education Department, 1990.

Oliver, L. P. *Study Circles: Coming Together for Personal Growth and Social Change.* Cabin John, Md.: Seven Locks Press, 1987.

Sharan, Y. "Group Investigation Expands Cooperative Learning." *Educational Leadership*, 1989–1990, *47* (4), 17–1.

Sheridan, J. "Collaborative Learning." *College Teaching*, 1989, *37* (2), 49–53.

Study Circles Resource Center. *An Introduction to Study Circles.* Pomfret, Conn.: Study Circles Resource Center, 1990.

Vestland, G. *How Do We Care for Democracy?* Stockholm, Sweden: National Swedish Board of Education, 1981.

Woodside, J. H. "Myles Horton: Pushing the Boundaries." *Now and Then: The Appalachian Magazine*, 1990, *7* (3), 22–23.

Workers' Educational Association. *Workers' Education in Sweden.* Stockholm, Sweden: ABS, 1973.

*LEONARD P. OLIVER directs Oliver Associates in Washington, D.C. Formerly, he was special assistant to the chair, National Endowment for the Humanities. He is currently staff associate with the Kettering Foundation and executive director of the Labor/Higher Education Council.*

*The "portable skills" developed through the process of learning in
the liberal arts—persistence, communications, critical thinking,
negotiating, planning, problem solving—enhance individuals in all
of their life roles and have particular applicability to the workplace.*

# Liberal Learning and the
# World of Work

*L. Steven Zwerling*

Before attempting to sketch an outline of ways in which liberal learning
fosters processes of self-development that can assist individuals throughout
their working lives, I wish to raise questions about some of the traditional
assumptions that influence current practice in adult and continuing education. The plan I propose will, in part, emerge from a critique of these
assumptions as it attempts to urge adult and continuing education in a
number of new directions.

## Questions

The earliest manifestations of adult education in the United States emphasized access, self-improvement, Americanization, voluntary participation,
and the wide distribution of culture and learning. Examples of this include
Ben Franklin's Junto, the Lowell and Cooper institutes, the Lyceum movement, the YMCA, the Chautauqua movement, settlement houses, and the
Cooperative Extension Service. Later, when colleges and universities and
business and industry came to dominate the field, access became limited:
what had been voluntary became de facto compulsory, and what had
encouraged assimilation became exclusive.

What role is adult and continuing education playing today with regard
to personal growth or social and economic equality? Does it contribute to
social mobility, development of individual potential, economic justice, meri-
tocracy? Or does it foster inequality, even economic and social regression?
My view is that adult and continuing education may in fact act as a regressive force in our society.

NEW DIRECTIONS FOR ADULT AND CONTINUING EDUCATION, no. 53, Spring 1992 © Jossey-Bass Publishers

So much about adult and continuing education is positive: the growth in enrollments, the diversity of offerings, the varieties of learning options, and the opportunities to satisfy career needs. In addition, we continue to learn about how adults learn and develop new methods, such as andragogy, and new media continue to contribute to the emergence of the first learning society in the history of the planet.

However, there is little evidence that there has been any change in people's *relative* position in the social hierarchy in spite of the democratization of higher education. The society is just as unequal as at the turn of the century. Though there has been inflation of both incomes and credentials, there has been little actual upward mobility. Money spent to support education is expected to aid in an economic redistribution based upon merit and achievement. But, actually, as many have noted, there is a net flow from poorer citizens to the more affluent as the result of inequities in the tax and the educational systems.

Even the excitement about theories of adult development and about the ways that they can help improve services to adults generally ignores the unexamined consequences. We like that adult development theory asserts a kind of predictability to a hitherto random art. It also contributes to our own professionalism: we are "andragogs."

There are, however, questions, even problems. If what is said about adult learning and development is valid, then adult classes are more heterogeneous than anything ever before encountered by educators, as these classes are typically populated by students from twenty-five to eighty-five years of age, spanning all levels of adult development. In the face of this, what do we as andragogs do with them, even with our knowledge of adult learning?

Adult developmental psychology in its current state posits a model of adult growth that is almost entirely passive: one passes through the stages of life at predictable times, in predictable order. Active, assertive learning models become obsolete. Life now is an obstacle course. The aim is simply to get through with minimum trouble and pain. Failure is to be behind schedule. Any deviation from the norm derives from a pathological source. If something goes wrong, the individual is not responsible; something must be wrong with his or her psychological clock.

Developmentalism becomes an imperative. Change careers! Embark on new marriages via creative divorce! Cut ties to the past! All of this assumes a passive, conservative role for continuing education. At most, educators are needed to cheer people on, provide skills for what is inevitable. There is little possibility for social or personal change. The goal of adulthood is merely to survive.

Continuing education may represent the final institutionalization of all learning from preschool to hospices. Christopher Lasch calls this "educationalization," the process whereby all experience becomes a course

(1978, p. 153). Adult and continuing education can become a substitute for experience while ironically trying to prepare people for it. Far from preparing students to live authentically, the new learning has the potential to be disabling, leaving people unable to perform the simplest tasks without instruction—find a job, prepare a meal, meet people, have sex.

Instead of lifelong *learning*, we may find adults virtually coerced into lifelong *schooling*. This coercion, from both mandated continuing education and the social pressure to raise the level of credentialing (presumably in response to the rising level of skills required for most work), helps perpetuate current class and status distinctions.

In addition, the emphasis on current education and responsiveness to the local economy—added to the focus on short-term retraining and upgrading of vocational skills, purportedly to enable people to change careers four to six times during a lifetime—does little to foster social mobility. In these ways, continuing education may actually contribute to the maintenance of a floating labor force that in the guise of providing opportunities for career change actually encourages people to move about without arriving at a destination.

The challenge, then, to adult and continuing educators is to articulate a future for our profession that is more equitable; that is enfranchising; that promotes voluntary, more intrinsic forms of learning; that emphasizes *active* learning; and that responds appropriately to the realities people face in the world of work. At the same time, it must encourage the kind of education that enables people to progress and to become more vocationally flexible so they can successfully negotiate the inevitable shifts in the structure of the economy.

## Liberal Reeducation

Though the preponderance of continuing education programming currently centers around technical and career education, liberal education still seems to be the appropriate place to begin a reconsideration of our mission, as it historically occupies the central position within higher education. Traditionally, liberal studies in continuing education presents itself to the public as an array of separate courses in the humanities and social sciences. Each course stands alone, and an institution's listing of its liberal arts offerings is rarely integrated. Potential students are left to browse through the catalog looking for something interesting on Wednesday nights.

It is rarer still for students enrolling for the fall term to have any idea about what will be offered in the spring, a situation that obviously subverts any intention they might have to plan more than one term at a time. In fact, the administrator responsible for the program may also have no clear idea of what will be offered in the spring until well after the fall semester's program is set in type.

Usually, when we speak about the reeducation of adults, we are in fact speaking about retraining. Displaced teachers seeking to change careers return to school to learn computer operations. Computer operators take courses to upgrade their skills in order to become systems analysts. Underemployed industrial workers learn to be medical assistants.

Much less frequently do we speak about reeducation in the liberal arts, however. The needs here are less obvious, but they are, nonetheless, vitally important. There are literally millions of people who completed their undergraduate education since the Second World War who could benefit from a reimmersion in the liberal arts, either because they were "too young" to reap the benefits of a well-structured liberal education when they went to college or because they attended college at a time when the curriculum was in disarray. The idea of comprehensive general education was in disrepute, and graduates came away with little to help them integrate either human or their own personal histories.

In addition, many more recent graduates opted for specialized, career-focused undergraduate programs; they are now coming to realize that, to advance in their jobs, they need the analytical and the critical-thinking skills provided by a liberal education. It is these adults who present a challenging new mission for continuing education.

In the 1950s and 1960s, educators were not reluctant to assert that to be well educated (or "well rounded") a person should be exposed to the major thinkers through the great books, or at least a selection of them. That carefully constructed undergraduate curriculum was designed for seventeen- and eighteen-year-olds who were often too young to appreciate the pageant of Western and non-Western civilization. Today, many of those graduates think about what they missed and dream of pulling out their old reading lists to encounter once again Aristotle, Jane Austin, and Charles Darwin now that they are experienced enough, sufficiently touched by life, to benefit from a college education.

The undergraduate of the late 1960s and early 1970s participated in challenging authority—academic authority included. The curriculum they helped shape was a smorgasbord that invited one to sample a little of this and a little of that. Many, in effect, majored in experience. Graduates of that era, who are now in their thirties and forties and trying to build careers, frequently express the need for a frame of reference for what they learned—or did not learn. People who took such courses as "The Contemporary American Novel" or "Nineteenth-Century Woman Writers," but never had a literature course that surveyed historical periods or literary criticism itself, are unlikely to have either the chronological framework or the analytical skills to make sense of what they experienced during their undergraduate years.

A third group consists of recent graduates still in their twenties; these young adults went to college with sharply defined career interests but have come to realize that their education lacked the breadth that they now recognize as important to their careers and to a fulfilled life. To them, career interests are appropriately still central; however, as they attempt to negotiate the middle levels of management, they are discovering that something is missing in their background, something that might be acquired through a return to liberal studies.

Programs for people in these three groups should consist of clusters of courses that connect in a meaningful way with one another over a number of semesters, in chronological groupings, around themes, about problems. They could be organized in more or less traditional academic configurations, in interdisciplinary arrangements, by genre, or in pursuit of specific communication and cognitive skills. No approach is mutually exclusive; successful programs could be structured according to more than one organizational principle. For example, the theme of world culture can be approached chronologically through a series of interdisciplinary courses and seminars.

A more traditional idea would be to trace the essence of the undergraduate comprehensive general-education requirements of such institutions as Columbia College and the University of Chicago. An adult and continuing education approach to this would allow students to live out the fantasy of rereading their college texts as mature adults and would satisfy the needs of many now in their middle years.

Adults often prefer a problem-centered curriculum in which academic content is framed by issues vital to their lives. It would not be difficult to shape a series of interdisciplinary courses that over a year or two would trace the human endeavor to consider such issues. History, philosophy, literature, and psychology, for example, would all lend their methods and discoveries to the courses.

More challenging would be to construct an appropriately organized grouping of courses that would satisfy the interests of recent, career-educated graduates. Modern professionals are realizing that they need more than technical competence. The focus for them should be on analytical and problem-solving skills, oral and written communication, and modes of negotiation in our and other cultures, coupled with some exposure to the humanities and social sciences. Such a curriculum might create two categories from which students could select their courses—one emphasizing skills that have direct professional application and one offering academic experiences that would fill in gaps in the student's educational background.

Though I earlier indicated a number of concerns about the sometimes misapplication of adult development theory to continuing education practice, I have often found it useful to test the comprehensiveness of an institution's liberal studies offerings against some of the implications of that theory. If one hypothesizes, for example, that there are indeed important differences in motivation and learning style that are a natural part of each life stage, one can look at a school's offerings to see if there are enough programs appropriate to potential students at different points in their lives.

One might devise a liberal studies planning matrix (Table 9.1) to analyze the offerings along these lines (Chickering, 1981; Morstain and Smart, 1974). The horizontal axis could delineate five stages in an adult life: early adulthood (twenty-three to thirty-five), midlife transition (thirty-five to forty-five), middle adulthood (forty-five to fifty-seven), late adult transition (fifty-seven to sixty-five), and late adulthood (over sixty-five); these are obviously driven by the force of time. The vertical axis would trace different, generally hierarchical, levels of motivation, moving in a developmental sequence from lower to higher, from extrinsic to intrinsic. Beginning with the lower developmental (and more externally motivated) levels of motivation, these would include expectations of a formal authority, career advancement to attain higher status, development of social relationships to fulfill desire for associations and friendships, services to humankind and to the community, escape or stimulation activities to break the routine and relieve boredom, personal development for self-improvement and increased personal happiness, and cognitive or cultural development to satisfy an inquiring mind and a need for a reflective, more philosophical perspective. The interaction of the horizontal and vertical axes of this matrix would tend to overlap at each level.

A theoretically "ideal" distribution or density of liberal studies offerings in a comprehensive program would reveal a lower distribution of liberal studies courses for those at the lower developmental, more extrinsically motivated, end of the matrix, and a progressively greater diversity of liberal studies courses at the higher developmental levels. As adults move through the stages of life, they are motivated more and more by intrinsic rewards. Thus, young adults are attracted to experiences that yield external payoffs, whereas older adults tend to seek learning for its own sake. Young adults are more likely to want to learn a foreign language for business purposes, less inclined to want to study history or philosophy. Thus, an institution located in an area with significant numbers of older adults could create programs appropriate to these potential students. If one finds a disproportionate number of thirty-five to forty-five-year-olds enrolled, chances are that the distribution of offerings would reflect this situation. One could then design new programs in appealing areas to serve additional audiences.

## A Look at Career Education

In the past, having an education meant getting a good job. Now, continuing one's education often means keeping a job. We can look at education for work in historical perspective. Initially, there was on-the-job training—essentially the only form of work-related education until this century. Next came prework preparation for work. The best example is the use of man-

# Table 9.1. Liberal Studies Planning Matrix

*Intrinsic* ←——————————————————————————————→ *Extrinsic*

| | Life Stage/Motivation | | | | |
|---|---|---|---|---|---|
| | *Early Adulthood (23–35)* | *Midlife Transition (35–45)* | *Middle Adulthood (45–57)* | *Late-Adult Transition (57–65)* | *Late Adulthood (65+)* |
| Cognitive/Cultural Interests | X | X X<br>X | X X X<br>X X X | X X X X<br>X X X X | X X X X X X<br>X X X X X X |
| Personal Fulfillment | X<br>X | X X<br>X | X X X X<br>X X X | X X X X<br>X X X X | X X X X X<br>X X X X X |
| Escape/Stimulation | X X<br>X | X X<br>X X | X X X X<br>X X X X X | X X X X<br>X X X X | X X X X<br>X X X |
| Citizenship | X X<br>X | X X<br>X X X | X X X X<br>X X X X X | X X X X<br>X X X | X X X X X<br>X X |
| Social Relationships | X X<br>X | X<br>X X X | X X X X<br>X X | X X X<br>X X | X X X<br>X |
| Professional Advancement | X<br>X | X X<br>X | X<br>X | X | X |
| External Expectations | X | X<br>X | X | X | X |

*Sources:* Adapted from Chickering, 1981; Morstain and Smart, 1974.

datory schooling as the virtually exclusive form of preparation. A third stream has now emphasized nonmandatory education for continuous career development. The pattern here is not unlike the second phase (prework preparation for work) but with the added educational dimension for career change, refinement, updating, and enhancement.

Though we assume that many adults move through what might be called normal career stages that correspond to levels of educational attainment— from kindergarten to postprofessional, from preemployment to retirement— more and more people do not live in this culture of expectations: people do not necessarily gain in employment status as they acquire more education. We encounter people who range from undereducated to overeducated. We see people who are underemployed or unemployed, fully employed or overemployed. We find that there are frames of reference and expectations associated with different combinations of educational level and employment status.

As educators, we tend to create programs in fewer than half of the potential areas of opportunity. Examining the parameters of conventional programming reveals potential new areas of opportunity. For the unemployed/ undereducated, we offer job training. For the underemployed/overeducated, we provide retraining and career redirection programs. For the employed/ undereducated, we present skills development and career enhancement opportunities. And for the employed/educated, we offer very little. The demographic crunch, slow economic growth, the micro-processing revolution, and the increasing divisions between rich and poor have created an environment of irregularity and unpredictability that has undermined the notion of clear career paths: we have messengers with M.B.A.'s, clericals with M.A.'s, computer programmers who were school dropouts, and rich people who are illiterate.

Adult and continuing educators have responded creatively *but incompletely*. Of course, matters are more complex than the analysis thus far would indicate. To serve the unemployed/educated or overeducated depends as much upon their ability to finance their participation as upon the availability of courses; moreover, to create programs for the overemployed at all educational levels demands the utmost skill.

Perhaps in seeming contradiction to my view that traditional, linear assumptions about career development only pertain to some, it may still be useful to look at theoretically conceived career stages to gain perspective on some new possibilities for adult and continuing career education. My perspective here is to look at the *generic* skills required at different career stages; it is in this way, I feel, that one can find ways to fill some of the empty spaces in a curriculum.

The opportunities present themselves to us when we concentrate on the *processes* people employ when making their way along a career path rather than on the specific instrumental *content* of their day-to-day work.

For our purposes, it is more important to look at the kinds of communication skills required for a middle-level systems analyst than at the person's need for specific knowledge of computers. Though it is appropriate for adult and continuing educators to provide courses in the specific content of systems analysis, to educate beyond traditional boundaries, we must look at the teachable skills that cross all specific content areas. Ironically, then, an examination of the generic competencies required at traditional steps along a "normal" career path (though that path exists less and less these days) leads educators into new areas that speak both to the needs of people pursuing a conventional track and to those of people who seem to be wandering.

If we investigate the skills essential at entry, mid-, and late-career stages, we find, for example, that entry-level skills for success, such as effective communications and data assimilation, are more specific, instrumental, technical. At midcareer, generic and general management skills, including planning, forecasting, problem-solving, and networking abilities, are required. And at the late-career stage, leadership and what some call "multidimensional" skills (like synthesizing, decision making, and mentoring) are important.

To move from stage to stage in the "normal" progression, individuals need to acquire what I call "next-step skills," during those times Havighurst (1972) calls "teachable moments." For example, moving from entry level to midcareer is aided by the acquisition of planning and forecasting skills, executive communications abilities, data management capabilities, and refined intuitive- and analytic-thinking capacities. To then move to a successful late career, midcareer individuals benefit from such next-step skills as the ability to manage via imaginative leadership, the capacity to persuade important public constituencies, and the skill necessary to make decisions and solve problems in multidimensional contexts.

As one can see, there are opportunities for various educational providers at different points along the way. Clearly, there is a major role for adult and continuing education at critical moments. And if one concentrates on the transmission of those most general skills, while at the same time continuing to offer viable courses and programs in more specific content areas, we can address the needs of adults moving along traditional career paths as well as of those who through choice or circumstance must find their own idiosyncratic ways.

## A Comprehensive Synthesis

Someone suggested that, in spite of current pressures, we should not go back to the basic three R's; instead, we should move on to the five C's: communications, computation, computer literacy, critical thinking, and collaboration. Though not necessarily the best formulation, the five C's seem one possible place to begin to look for a comprehensive synthesis of liberal and career studies that will assist us in adding to our traditional continuing education armories the new, nonprogressive, dialectical, discontinuous programs of action *and* expectation that people require to be viable in contemporary society.

When the CEO talks about the need to produce "work-ready" people, he or she is urging that we set limits to the degrees of specialization that we educators seek to engender. We must think about the durability and adaptability of the skills and attitudes that we attempt to provide to students.

When I was asked recently to deliver a talk on career trends in the 1990s, I only half facetiously replied that I felt more confident talking about career trends in the 1890s than the 1990s. As personnel forecasting is notable mainly for its errors, I emphasized the need to acquire portable abilities—flexibility, persistence, communications, thinking, negotiating, planning, problem solving—the skills of successful people.

In addition, the old cliché that "a good (liberal) education is wasted on the young" may, in fact, be true. The psychic tasks that need to be accomplished, the major events that rather predictably mark their lives, the fundamental needs and learning styles of the young, do not contribute to the kind of integrative learning fundamental to the assumptions of an undergraduate education. Traditional-age students are not ready for the kinds of "front-loaded" general education curricula that form the core of the first two postsecondary years. Ironically, though continuing education is generally the lowest-status function of colleges and universities, in this context it may be that the most appropriate role for a college is to be a center for lifelong learning.

It may also be that, through continuing education, liberal and career education will be more likely to blend than in other more rigidly structured parts of higher education. Perhaps here we will transcend the discussion that places liberal and career education in two separate cultures: the best *liberal* education may come to be seen as career education; the best *career* education may be seen to be liberal education.

One example of this possible synthesis involves career educators who have recently turned some of their attention to the management of crises. Faced with the realities of overseas competition, financially ailing banks, product failures, unfriendly takeover attempts, the adverse impact of world events on the price of crude oil, and other crises, a number of industrial and corporate leaders look for qualities in managers that enable them to lead in difficult times. In these contexts, they look to creative people who can handle ambiguity. When one attempts to teach the skills of creative leadership, one generally utilizes texts such as *The Competent Manager* (Boyatzis, 1982) or organizes exercises that simulate organizational crises. An additional, admittedly less-tested approach that might further executives' ability to deal with ambiguity involves study in the humanities. There may be no better place to discover the complexities of crises *and* the characteristics of the various, and successful, attempts to grapple with them. Stanford University's and the Aspen Institute's programs for business leaders, for instance, see an intensive immersion in the humanities as yielding more than intrinsic satisfactions: there are significant functional benefits.

To implement a comprehensive program based upon these principles, it may be useful to develop a chart to serve as a guide (see Table 9.2). The horizontal axis is again organized according to life stages. The vertical one this time delineates the major milestones and psychic tasks for each stage in the life cycle, as well as the learning styles generally favored by adults during these different phases. In addition, I would suggest including appropriate learning formats and programmatic responses that speak to the psychological needs and practical realities of people at various points in their lives.

To indicate how this chart might be helpful, consider a vertical column for middle adulthood. This is a time in life when individuals traditionally attain the summit of their careers, become mentors to younger colleagues, see their children establish autonomous lives, develop new interests, become more involved in community events, and deal with inevitable physical limitations. In the psychic realm, it is usual to reexamine the relationship between one's circumstances and changing sense of self. People tend to become increasingly self-aware and, after having reassessed family relationships, either reaffirm them or seek new ones.

Because of physiological and psychological changes, because of the accumulation of experience from their professional and personal lives, people during middle adulthood tend to seek interactive or expressive modes of learning. Much of it is self-directed. Mediated learning, however, tends to be best when it draws heavily on that accrued experience. As learners, adults at this stage of life often seek collegial affiliations with both their co-learners and their instructors. Short formats are often best if the content is informational. Longer, seminar formats are appropriate for more inner-directed study.

Programmatic responses for people of this age could involve career updates in multidimensional contexts: technical advances *plus* ethical issues and considerations; issues in business *plus* historical and cultural foundations; regulatory issues *plus* sociological perspectives. The desire for personal self-examination and integration could involve seminars and discussion groups that explore the life cycle itself as revealed in literature, psychology, and the biographies of historical figures. Membership groups in either public or community affairs could satisfy some of the desire for affiliation, continued professional networking, and the development of new interests to fill the later years.

Clearly, there is the opportunity here for appropriate, separate career and liberal programming. However, there is the additional opportunity for

# Table 9.2. A Comprehensive Program in Continuing Education

| | Early Adulthood (23–35) | Midlife Transition (35–45) | Middle Adulthood (45–57) | Late-Adult Transition (57–65) | Late Adulthood (65+) |
|---|---|---|---|---|---|
| **Programmatic Responses** | Training for career advancement<br>Career planning/pathing workshops<br>Paraprofessional programs<br>Marriage/parenting workshops<br>Sports/recreation<br>Stress management<br>Civic education/volunteer training<br>Personal finance | Mid-career assessment<br>Retraining for unemployed<br>Career change workshops<br>Integrated liberal studies<br>Social science/science courses<br>Sports/recreation<br>Consumer education<br>Living alone/divorce workshops<br>Parents' and children's programs<br>Values clarification/goal-setting workshops<br>Personal financial planning<br>Stress management<br>Reentry programs (esp. for women) | Executive programming<br>Career updates<br>Membership groups<br>Education for community leadership<br>Public affairs programs<br>Integrated liberal studies<br>Social science and science programs<br>Sponsored travel—culture, language, cuisine<br>Cultural programs<br>Consumer education<br>Stress management | Executive mentoring programs<br>Pre-retirement workshops<br>Public affairs programs (national/international)<br>Personal health and nutrition<br>Arts, writing, music courses<br>Cultural programs<br>Sponsored travel<br>Money management/estate planning<br>Consumer education<br>Workshops on aloneness, death and dying<br>Courses in philosophy and religion | Membership groups for seniors<br>Public affairs programs<br>Cultural programs<br>Elderhostel<br>Money management<br>Consumer education<br>Religious and philosophical exploration<br>Death and dying workshops<br>Health and nutrition programs |
| **Learning Styles and Formats** | Specialization focus<br>Instrumental orientation—direct relevance<br>Unidimensional thinking<br>Integrate academic study with career experiences<br>Emphasize short-term goals<br><br>Flexible schedules—weekend, intensive programs<br>Distance learning<br>Experiential learning<br>Classroom-based learning | Specialization still dominates<br>Begin balance between instrumental and expressive educational orientation<br>Assess and build on prior learning<br><br>Counseling and advising<br>Individualized approaches: contracts, independent study, distance learning<br>Flexible schedules and formats<br>Life experience credit<br>Workshops and classroom-based learning | Desire for integration<br>Balance toward expressive orientation<br>Multidimensional thinking<br>Draw heavily on life experience<br>Opportunities for collegial relationships with faculty<br><br>Life experience credit<br>One- and two-day formats<br>Discussion groups<br>Forums<br>Conferences, workshops, seminars<br>Simulations | Integration<br>Philosophical/religious orientation<br><br>Access to study (off campus programs)<br>Discussion groups<br>Forums<br>Workshops<br>Studio courses | |

| | | | | | |
|---|---|---|---|---|---|
| **Psychic Tasks** | Establish autonomy and independence from family<br>Define identity<br>Establish new peer alliances<br>Regard self as adult<br>Develop capacity for intimacy<br>Fashion adult life-style<br>Define one's dream<br>Find a mentor<br>Reappraise relationships<br>Reexamine life-style and commitments<br>Strive for success<br>Search for stability, security, control<br>Search for personal values<br>Set long-range goals<br>Accept growing children | Face reality<br>Confront mortality<br>Prune dependent ties to boss, spouse, mentor<br>Reassess marriage<br>Reassess priorities and values | Increase feelings of self-awareness and competence<br>Reestablish family relationships<br>Enjoy one's choices and life-style<br>Reexamine fit between life circumstances and sense of self | Accomplish goals in time left to live<br>Accept and adjust to aging process | Search for meaning (integrity) instead of despair<br>Accept self<br>Disengagement<br>Rehearsal for death of spouse and self |
| **Market Events** | Marry<br>Establish/manage home<br>Become parent<br>Get hired/fired<br>Enter community activities<br>Children in school<br>Progress in/change in career<br>Possible separation/divorce<br>Possible return to school | Critical promotion<br>Break with mentor<br>Responsibility for three-generation family: growing children, aging parents<br>For women: empty nest, reenter career and education | Cap career<br>Become mentor<br>Launch children; become grandparent<br>New interests and hobbies<br>Physical limitations; menopause<br>Active participation in community events | Possible loss of mate<br>Health problems<br>Prepare for retirement | Retirement/relocation<br>Physical decline<br>Change in finances<br>Dependent on children<br>Death of friends/spouse<br>Major shift in daily routine |

*Sources:* Chickering and Havighurst (1982); Cross (1981); Lehman and Lester (1978); Levinson and others (1974); McCoy, Ryan, and Lictenberg (1978); Neugarten (1968); Weathersby (1978).

programming that spans this traditional division. And there are equivalent possibilities at all other life stages. It may also be that these new opportunities are among the best for educators who aspire to meet the comprehensive, complex needs of adults.

## Equity

Earlier, I speculated that adult and continuing education may inadvertently act as a regressive force in society—that it is potentially the most unequal form of organized educational activity. Ironically, it simultaneously has the potential to play the *most* progressive role. It is certain that having a good education encourages people to continue to learn; and unlike other forms of study, continuing education for the most part is accessible to all. It generally does not formally admit the students that it enrolls; most courses and programs, for example, allow mail and telephone registration. There are few prerequisites other than an individual's motivation and confidence that she or he can do the work.

It would, of course, be naive to assume casually that everyone would feel confident about their ability to succeed in programs of continuing education—especially those who did not fare well in their previous schooling. Acknowledging these psychological and cultural barriers, however, does not detract from the clear evidence that many kinds of people can and do succeed academically when they do participate.

Equity then requires that we do a better job of reaching out. This is a complicated objective and necessitates, among other things, the commitment of resources and development of programs. It also means dealing with people's consciousness of the relationship between different forms of education and the quality of their lives.

In previous years, many thought that being a high school graduate would adequately enhance their career chances and enrich their lives in other less tangible ways. Later, many came to conclude that a college degree was the credential that would lead to the opportunities they sought. More recently, many have pursued graduate and professional degrees for the same reasons. Most recently, there is the belief among many that lifelong learning is a key to a successful and rich life.

In some communities, however, it is still felt that the college degree is the critical credential. Though obviously important in itself, it rarely any longer leads to the kinds of rewards envisioned. Indeed, many adults who earn an undergraduate degree later in life are disappointed when they discover it does not automatically offer access to new or improved careers. They encounter age discrimination certainly, but they also find that employers are looking for more than the "piece of paper"; they seek kinds of competencies best gained via continuing education.

Thus, people in communities who have traditionally been bypassed, in spite of the expansion of educational opportunities, have the chance to use the new opportunities presented by continuing education to their own advantage. If they can come to understand this shifting history of the relationship between levels of education and career and life enhancement, they can enter directly and immediately that sector of education currently offering the richest rewards.

The most substantial barriers to access are actually those of our own devising. This is both the bad news and the good. Ultimately, the picture must be viewed optimistically, as the solutions to the problems that must be overcome rest in our hands.

## References

Boyatzis, R. E. *The Competent Manager.* New York: Wiley, 1982.
Chickering, A. W., and Associates. *The Modern American College: Responding to the New Realities of Diverse Students and a Changing Society.* San Francisco: Jossey-Bass, 1981.
Havighurst, R. J. *Developmental Tasks and Education.* (3rd ed.) New York: McKay, 1972.
Lasch, C. *The Culture of Narcissism.* New York: Norton, 1978.
Morstain, B. R., and Smart, J. C. "Reasons for Participation in Adult Education Courses: A Multivariate Analysis of Group Differences." *Adult Education,* 1974, 24 (2), 83-98.

*L. STEVEN ZWERLING is program officer in the Division of Education and Culture at the Ford Foundation. Prior to that he was associate dean of New York University's School of Continuing Education. He is the author of* Second-Best: The Crisis of the Community College *(McGraw-Hill),* The Community College and Its Critics *(Jossey-Bass), and the forthcoming* First-Generation Students: Confronting the Cultural Issues.

*This chapter summarizes key elements discussed throughout the book and distills them to provide useful information and practical recommendations for adult educators.*

# Concluding Notes: A Direction for Learning

*Angela Sgroi, Lorraine A. Cavaliere*

In this last chapter, we offer some observations of the learning that can lead to personal development. We were asked by fellow adult educators if there was a way to "bottle the magic" of this learning. We hope that we have been able to capture and identify at least some of it here.

Following the pattern established in Chapter One, we will organize these observations around the concepts of self, context, and integration of the two. We then offer suggestions to the adult educator derived from these observations.

## Observations of the Self

Chapter after chapter in this sourcebook (and similarly in most other accounts of learning for personal development) makes it clear that the primary motivation for learning is based on following the dictates of some internal voice. Carr addresses it directly when he refers to "the subjectivity of learning." The social advocates portrayed by Williams, Cavaliere's depiction of the Wright brothers, the older dancers figuring in Sgroi's chapter, and the senior citizens who engage in learning activities described by Wolf are all moving through uncertain terrain driven by some internal force. Understanding the internal mandate, Oliver argues that the study circle provides a powerful mechanism for intrinsically motivated learning goals.

Cavaliere quotes Wilber Wright, who says that he is "afflicted with the belief that flight is possible to man." Wolf cites the "readiness" that older learners experience for meaning-making through their learning experiences;

they are often developing something that has always been a part of themselves but has been left undeveloped so far.

The aspects of the self emerge in different ways in the chapters in this book as internal compulsions, needs, or mandates that seem to motivate the initiation of the learning. This section examines the elements of identity, emotion, self-assertion and meaning-making, a learning response to failure, and a set of particular capabilities unique to these learners.

**Identity.** The learner's identity is a critical element in the learning process, whether it is the motivation for learning something one is fascinated with, learning about oneself through the process of understanding some particular problem, or undertaking that particular learning as a means of identifying, affirming, or extending one's identity as a human being (Aristotle's daimon) (Waterman, 1990). Carr is adamant about this: "Identity is critical to inquiry."

Williams's definition of action learning is a questioning of "the basic tenets and assumptions through a nonnormative life event." He sees the continuing self-definition manifest itself through a process of "testing old rules." The social advocates all reported "asking difficult questions of themselves" about personal beliefs and actions. He notes: "In all cases I have examined, action learning involved some challenge to common perceptions or current paradigms of thinking."

The Wrights' personal vision changed the world. The dancers changed their own assumptions and those of their audiences about how beauty, grace, and expressiveness in dance are defined.

**Emotion.** Because it derives from a personal drive, learning for personal development is often accompanied by strong emotions. These will often propel the learner over what might otherwise be insurmountable obstacles. At the very least, this emotional investment helps the learner to maintain a strong interest in the subject and may help account for the unyielding persistence in learning described in many of the chapters.

Certainly, this level of passion for subject or problem and for the learning needed to understand the subject or solve the problem is apparent in all of the social advocates. It is evident in the Wright brothers and the dancers. As Christopher Lasch says: "When we get into arguments that focus and fully engage our attention, we become avid seekers of relevant information" (1991, p. 72).

**Self-Assertion and Meaning Making.** This idea of being in search of self, of seeking visibility as affirmation of one's own real existence, is not new. Ralph Ellison's *The Invisible Man* (1947), although written about the experience of the black person in this society, has become a classic because it describes that sense of invisibility that we all feel.

Many of the learners described in this book seem to be striving for meaning in the larger sense of trying to understand their lives. So the learning is not only a fulfilling of personal goals, but also a process of identifying the overall pattern and direction of one's life. Both Wolf and Zwerling identify this search primarily with older adulthood. Wolf tells us, "Older learners are often led into adult education by a quest for self-development and the wish to make meaning of the human experience."

**A Learning Response to Failure.** Depending on the particular personality qualities of the learner and the intensity of the motivation for a particular learning experience, failure can serve to spur on the learning. Cavaliere has built failure into her model of learning. Langer and Brown recommend it as a strategy: "A mindful look at failure reveals that, if we change the context and look at it from a different perspective, we may remove the failure."

**A Particular Set of Learner Qualities.** Any observations of adult learning must always include recognition of the nature of the adult learner. This discussion will focus only on those particular qualities that are apparent in adults learning for personal development and that are not common to other forms of adult learning. Some of these are (1) keen awareness of self and context, (2) ability to tolerate ambiguity, (3) willingness to take risks, (4) a predisposition to reflective thinking, (5) knowledge of self and personal learning style, and (6) a high level of persistence.

In summary, we have seen that, as the drive for learning emerges from an inner compulsion, these people have taken control of their environment and often changed their perspectives en route. The process seems to yield strong emotions that heighten motivation and persistence. Also worth noting is a positive role for failure and some unique qualities of learners in these learning situations.

## Observations of the Context

The context is made up of anything outside of the learner that influences the learning in some way. Some of the aspects of context include cultural and subcultural world view, values, beliefs and standards, local and historical setting, the organization of space and time, the availability of resources, knowledge and time, people, the marginality of the learner, and the influence of contextual structures.

Three elements of context that stand out in the works in this volume are people, the marginality of the learner, and the influence of contextual structures.

**People.** For all of our contributors, interaction with mentors, peers, partners, citizens in the community, information sources, master teachers, authors, museum curators, and the like provides a powerful contextual influence on personal learning.

Even in cultural institutions, there is interaction with authorities who are witnesses to events, even though they are not physically present. Cavaliere demonstrates the mentor role played by Octave Chanute, but she also discusses a less frequently studied interaction: the power of the partner, which, for the Wright brothers, may have been one of the major driving factors toward success. Sgroi discusses the role of the teacher as pivotal in the development of many of the dancers. The dance teacher is something like a mentor, but more like the oriental master-teacher, showing values and culture, as well as skill and knowledge.

Wolf, too, has observed the incredible power that a teacher can have, but she also talks about the increasing importance of connectedness for older learners—"a need to touch and be part of the world. It is a fear of human loss, of impoverishment. We can say, 'I am awake; I am here.'"

The study circle, according to Oliver, relies on the gregarious nature of humans. They work because people make connections with, challenge, respond to, teach, and learn from other people.

**Marginality.** A number of the authors mention marginality of the learner to a situation or to society as a contributor to learning. Marginality as described by Williams, Cavaliere, and Wolf seems to be one phenomenon that forces the mindful state defined by Langer and Brown. Cavaliere describes how the Wrights worked primarily outside of all established systems—they were geographically remote, outside of the scientific circle, excluded from most information networks (except for their link with Chanute). Could their marginality have stimulated the creation of new ideas that led to flight?

Williams indicates, "Whereas deprivation appears to be a negative influence on development, empowerment, and social activism, marginality seems to be liberating." It gives a person the experience and perspective of more than one culture and opens the way for new insights. "It is this tradition of marginality that distinguishes the advocates from many of their ethnic, socioeconomic, and cultural peers. They had experienced or witnessed possibilities of other cultures, becoming in the process 'the discontent dancing with hope.'"

For Wolf, marginality is the result of a long life for many older adults. They straddle cultures quite often because they lived a long time, and their varied experiences over time created different mindsets.

**Influence of Contextual Structures.** For Williams's social advocates, these structures were usually governmental or bureaucratic, and they frequently created obstacles that the advocates generally treated as challenges to be circumvented or overcome (as many learners treated failures). Overcoming obstacles had to do with the perspective of the learner and often inspired learning, as discussed by Langer and Brown. Carr's discussion shows the extent to which context can be exploited and positively structured to enhance learning.

## Observations of the Integration of Self and Context

We can see that we live in a time of extraordinarily rapid and dramatic change. This situation creates an even greater need for individuals constantly to redefine themselves. Change, of course, when met head on, usually necessitates learning.

Based on the frameworks presented by Rogoff (1990) and Vygotsky (1978), we will examine the critical elements of learning when self and context are integrated. In this section, we will discuss action, dynamic process, goal-driven process, and transformations.

**Action.** Action is at the heart of learning for personal development. The learning itself is active. It is always moving, changing direction, leaping to unexpected places. At the same time, it requires action from the learner. Williams characterizes the learning of the social advocates as "action learning." In order to learn about aerodynamics and flight in their efforts to invent the airplane, the Wrights had to be physically active in the process, jumping off of cliffs on gliders or constructing models by hand.

If the structures for cognitive change within individuals described by Carr are engaged by the design of institutions, that engagement is initiated by the action of the individual. The older learners described by Wolf do primarily attend classes in formal learning situations, but the search for meaning that she describes comes about for many of these people through their active participation in the process. The adult dancers are physically active, but it is their mental activity while moving that makes learning dance meaningful and more than just a physical workout.

At the core of mindfulness is action: active observation, active discrimination, and active and constant analysis and synthesis. Langer and Brown's concept of conditional learning and conditional teaching encompasses the awareness that learning—indeed, that our perception of what occurs in life—is constantly changing, open to multiple interpretations, shifting directions.

**Dynamic Process.** Learning for personal development emerges as primarily a vastly dynamic process in which the self changes in response to a constantly evolving context; and as the self changes, the perception of the content changes. Therefore, when Williams talks about action learning, he carefully points out that people describe a process whereby they understand what they are thinking by acting on their thoughts. They "act out the emerging mental construct in both its positive and negative aspects. . . . [They act out] to create more dimensions for their [the advocates] new role." There is a "creation of new paradigms (or perceptual sets) that are shaped by the positive aspects of old paradigms." Action learners interviewed say "they are 'acting out' concepts that remain poorly formed in thoughts and inadequately described in words."

Williams's description of the dynamic seems to capture it well: "The construction of new perceptual sets seemed to grow, with some difficulty, out of new 'expectancies,' . . . new 'direct or vicarious opportunities,' . . . and even out of new dreams or imagination." Sometimes a critical event triggered the change. Always, it was accompanied by strong positive or negative emotion.

We see the pattern again and again in this kind of learning—in the dancers, for the Wrights, in the older learners. They initiate the action. They involve themselves in something that then takes on a life of its own. At this point, it is generally impossible to distinguish the dancer from the dance, the self from the context. As each changes, it leads to change in the other.

**A Goal-Driven Process Orientation.** We have observed repeatedly that learning for personal development is active (as described above) and, therefore, basically process oriented. Each chapter, regardless of whether the individual author emphasized process or goal, encompasses both. Occasionally, the goals are broad and long-range (the dancers wanted to learn to dance), and some of the goals are very specific (achieving flight). In every case, however, these objectives drive a process that becomes a critical element contributing to the development of the learner, even when process was not his or her primary concern. Zwerling's notion of "portable skills," for example, recognizes that the process of learning under most circumstances will develop new skills that can serve the learning in many other aspects of life.

Some of the contributors describe common behaviors they observed in the process of learning for personal development. There are striking similarities in those processes described. Each includes some form of goal setting, focusing on the problem or activity, information gathering, thinking or reflecting, engaging in actions that further appropriate learning (such as skill development, practice, or Williams's concept of acting through the thinking process), persevering, evaluating, and reformulating.

**Transformations.** Dramatic changes can result when the individual and the environment or context come together in the right way, at the right time, and with sufficient passion or motivation. As a result of the Wright brothers, the world is changed forever. Society is also changed significantly. Consider the different path of history following the acts of Cesar Chavez, Albert Turner, Sr., Candy Lightner, or any of the other social advocates described by Williams. Study circles are being organized by congressmen and senators who want to understand the views and values of their constituencies; as a result, group collaboration will have a direct influence on the political processes.

Individuals are changed dramatically in the way they see and live. Wolf found that, for the institutionalized elderly, "attention span, locus of control, and selfhood can be revived through stimulating experiences [action]." She says, "We must shift our perceptions of how to nourish physically frail elders." Langer and Brown make very similar observations based on a different body of research.

**Concluding Observations.** Carr describes the process for learning in this personal way and, in doing so, offers a summary for this section of the chapter. "[Learning] experiences also enlarge the map of living. They add new boundaries to definitions, create greater depths of complexity discovered below the surfaces of life, identify additional authorities whose thinking must be understood, and provide fresh perspectives that lead to differing interpretations of the world. . . . These encounters may make difficult and problematic the knowledge we have previously used to keep on course. They change our understanding of self and human values; they shake our foundations."

## Applications for Adult Educators

What do these ideas mean for adult education? What are possible applications and adaptations? How can they be transferred, institutionalized? The learners described throughout this sourcebook are exploring, stretching, reaching, sometimes struggling to find ways to shape their world into their images—to understand and in some way control their reality.

Each chapter in this book presents rich insights and challenging notions about learning, most of which we have highlighted in this chapter. But what we consider to be the most valuable contributions of each author are the profound questions they elicit in our thinking. Langer and Brown set the pattern in Chapter Two with their proposal that all life be viewed conditionally. All of the chapters provoke serious examination of our metaphysical, epistemological, and axiological perspectives of learning. What is the essential nature of the aging adult? How do we know what we believe about adults and adult learning is true? What is "good" or "right" for others?

With the sovereignty of the learner over his or her own learning as a basic premise, we offer the following suggestions for consideration. Again, we point out that our recommendations will most likely represent a change in emphasis, not one in basic behaviors and process. The recommendations are grouped as follows: regard the individual, incorporate the influences of people, exploit the environment, ensure active involvement, assist in navigating the unknown, and develop a liberal studies curriculum.

**Regard the Individual.** Educators and educational institutions, in considering the critical nature of self to learning, might be advised to make the individual a central goal in designing the curriculum and learning experiences. Carr recommends undermining "anonymity, impersonality, distance. . . . the process of learning is the way toward a self-designed life." Simply knowing one's students—paying attention to them and commenting knowledgeably about learning behaviors—is an obvious, powerful means for teachers to establish trust and encourage learning. Langer and Brown recommend avoiding "premature cognitive commitments" when taking in new information about people and situations.

Oliver contends that there is an "absence of adult education mechanisms that emphasize the individual's views and need to be recognized." He argues for the study circle as a way to reveal the value of the individual.

"In mass meetings, in most classrooms, in our full-agenda, fast-paced world, individual experiences can often be overlooked, we never come to know each other, and the dialogue suffers."

**Incorporate the Influences of People.** The role of the teacher may be the most pivotal element of the context when it is a formal educational situation. Despite the obvious fact that we cannot give someone something they are unwilling to accept, the teacher can wield considerable influence, primarily by guiding the learner to opportunities for growth and by offering encouragement.

In the end, teachers must be willing to offer themselves to the learner. It is the passions, commitments, and values of the teachers that seem to be sought after by adult learners. Wolf talks about older people expecting their teachers to be "authentic." Sgroi found that dancers only attended the classes of teachers they trusted; these were people who respected their students, knew and loved their subject, and knew how to teach it. It follows then that teachers who see the magic in the subject that they teach are likely to pass that gift on to the learner.

Oliver argues, "Collaborative learning, through study circles, changes the usual teacher/professorial role of the expert dispensing knowledge to passive adult students. The study circle leader is . . . a guide to help adult learners to work together, to analyze problems jointly, to come up with common actions." In addition to utilizing the power of the group for learning, the teacher might wish to consider Cavaliere's suggestion concerning the power of partnerships for learning.

**Exploit the Environment.** The importance of contextual forces cannot be underestimated. What is the learning environment like? What resources are available? How does the prevailing cultural aspect of the learning environment influence the learning? How can it be improved? What information networks are available or can be made accessible to learners? For Langer and Brown, this might entail presenting aspects of the environment from multiple perspectives. Their idea of conditional teaching requires that we learn to view our world and our places in it in a variety of possible ways.

Carr's advice to educators is particularly interesting because it is intended for structuring learning environments in cultural institutions. Thus, educator and learner are not likely to come face-to-face. He says, "It is essential for educators to invest themselves in these unimaginable unknowns by creating appropriate conditions and situations for the right sparks to be struck and for the most flammable tinder to be touched by them." These conditions and situations are any aspects of the context that the teacher feels comfortable manipulating.

**Ensure Active Involvement.** The action of learning is easily facilitated by designing the kinds of hands-on, problem-solving situations recommended by Carr and others. An approach to instruction that encourages dialogue and challenges the conventional mindset, a method derived most frequently recently from Freire and Mezirow, sometimes assists learners in exploring their own values and actions.

**Assist in Navigating the Unknown.** Helping others to deal with the unknown is quite likely one of the most important kinds of support one individual can give to another. Teachers and educational institutions should build this assistance into all plans for learning. A teacher can help an individual to develop a variety of possible approaches to a problem, as well as continually to redefine and reconceive it. Langer and Brown encourage this method of teaching and learning. A fascinating curriculum might be one that centered experiences for learners around the idea of constant change and that found means of helping them perceive change in positive ways.

Such a liberating curriculum might encourage multiple views of a problem or situation, identify ways an event might be likely or unlikely, and show the positive, negative, or neutral aspects of an outcome. It might also encourage the making of models and replications of models, experimenting, practicing, and physically acting out ideas.

Encouraging intuitive knowledge and creative thought (Sgroi) in learning situations assists in the journey toward discovery of meaning or self by supporting the development of the tools that can be used to navigate the unknown.

**Develop a Liberal Studies Curriculum.** The notion of a personal exploration or journey brings to mind the spirit of the liberal education. This is education that intends to assist the individual in understanding the workings of the world on a grand scale and the individual's place in it. As a result, it generally includes learning about the physical world, the history of civilization, and human beings as they behave as individuals, as part of groups, and as citizens of a larger society.

We say the *spirit* of a liberal education because in practice it has tended to be elitist, to be taught through a teacher-oriented model, to be exclusionary, and to eschew the real-life problems that it is best prepared to attack. Our suggestion, then, is a model that maintains the aims of liberal education and uses a means of implementation that can more readily be classified within the progressive model. We call this combination a liberating curriculum.

Zwerling calls for a future for adult education "that is more equitable; that is enfranchising; that promotes voluntary, more intrinsic forms of learning; that emphasizes *active* learning; and that responds appropriately to the realities people face in the world of work. At the same time, it must encourage the kind of education that enables people to progress and to become more vocationally flexible so they can successfully negotiate the inevitable shifts in the structure of the economy."

He sees this goal being accomplished through liberal education. Reading from the known or recognized major thinkers has been considered an effective means for developing analytical and critical-thinking skills, an understanding of human nature, and the human experience needed in the workplace and in all aspects of life.

The broad knowledge base, concentration on theories and values, and process of analysis and critical thinking fostered in liberal studies programs as described by Zwerling also serve an individual well, especially in uncertain terrain.

Learning for personal development, because it is chosen by the individual, has many lessons for the educators. The intensity of the personal aspect of the learning, the powerful influence of all contextual factors, and the way that these forces interact provide us with useful guides in designing curricula and learning experiences in adult education.

Learning for personal development is the quest—a lifelong search for self. It is initiated by an internal compulsion, and nothing along the way is clear or certain. Learners find their way by feeling and intuition. They meet any number and type of obstacles along the way. If an obstacle is overcome, the individual grows and becomes stronger. If it is not, the journey is terminated or indefinitely delayed.

The difference between this quest and that of the Odysseus of legend is that these heroes are flesh-and-blood, everyday people. They are the people you meet in the supermarket and at football games. They work as brain surgeons and as dishwashers. They are teachers; they are students. They are you.

## References

Ellison, R. *The Invisible Man*. New York: New American Library, 1947.

Lasch, C. "The Art of Political Argument." *Utne Reader*, 1991, 44, 72–73.

Rogoff, B. *Apprenticeship in Thinking*. New York: Oxford University Press, 1990.

Vygotsky, L. S. *Mind in Society: The Development of Higher Psychological Processes*. Cambridge, Mass.: Harvard University Press, 1978.

Waterman, A. S. "Personal Expressiveness: Philosophical and Psychological Foundations." *Journal of Mind and Behavior*, 1990, 11 (1), 47–74.

ANGELA SGROI *is executive assistant to the vice president for academic affairs at Trenton State College in New Jersey.*

LORRAINE A. CAVALIERE *is director of continuing studies at Rutgers University.*

# INDEX

Abelson, R. P., 11
Acting out new concepts, 41–42
Action learning, 117; adult education encouragement of, 47–48; defining, 39–40; institutional barriers to, 46; a model for, 43–45; social advocates and, 37–50; steps in, 40–43
Actualizing stage, learning project, 56
Adams, J., 86
Adult education: encouragement of action learning by, 47–48; equity and, 99–100, 112–113; learning-teaching interaction in, 67–69; liberal arts graduate groups needing, 102–103; questioning the mission of, 99–101; as reeducation or retraining, 101–102
Age levels, adult, 74, 102–103; liberal studies planning for, 104–105
Aging, learning while, 38, 73–84
Airplane, invention of the, 51–59
Allport, G., 30
Ambiguity, tolerance for, 40, 108–109, 117
Andragogy, 100
Apprenticeship, cognitive, 27–30; interactive qualities of, 28
Art education, avocational, 61–71
Art forms: fascination with, 62–64; the process of learning, 64–67
Atkins, B. K., 81–82

Baltes, P. B., 80
Bandura, A., 40
Barnes, C., 64
Barriers, overcoming, 66
Beder, H., 56
Beiswanger, G., 63, 65
Birren, J. E., 76, 77
Blid, H., 86
Borodin, A., 61
Boyatzis, R. E., 108
Brandstadter, J., 38, 39–40
Brockett, R. G., 8, 68
Brookfield, S. D., 52, 54, 68
Brown, J. S., 28–29
Brubaker, E. B., 37, 38
Busch-Rossnagel, N. A., 40

Butler, R. N., 76
Butterfield, E. C., 42

Caffarella, R. S., 8
Caldicott, H., 39, 40
Candy, P. C., 8
Career stages: education levels and, 104–106; generic competencies and, 106–107; liberal education and, 107–112
Case study: of learning by social advocates, 37–50; of learning by the Wright brothers, 51–59
Certainty and mindlessness, 14–15
Change: action learning and, 38–39; behavior choice and, 18–19; cognitive, 27; as opportunity for learning, 11, 118–120, 121
Chanowitz, B., 12, 13
Chanute, O., 51, 55
Chavez, C., 39–40, 42, 44, 45, 46
Chickering, A. W., 104
Chiriboga, D. A., 78
Choice work, value-based, 90–91
Citizenship, study circles and democratic, 85–88
Civil rights action learning, 41–42
Clusters of courses, availability of, 101, 103
Cognition: apprenticeship and, 27–30; challenges toward, 25–27, 33, 43–45; learning and reordering, 78–80; repetitive processes of, 53–56
Cognitive commitments, premature, 14–15
Collaborative learning: dynamics, 88–91; in partnership, 57; in study circles, 87–92, 93–95
Collard, S., 47
Collins, A., 28–29
Combs, A. W., 43
Conditional learning, 14–15
Conditional learning and teaching, 119
Context of learning, 6; the apprenticeship, 27–30; the group or community, 32, 81–82, 90–96; independent, 51–59; influence of the, 56–57; institutional structures as the, 89–91, 118;

125

tory of, 85-86; as a small-group phe-
nomenon, 93
Success and failure, 16-19
Sweden, study circles in, 86, 92-93
Synthesis of liberal and career studies,
107-112

Taylor, S. E., 16
Teachers, roles of adult education, 67-
70, 80
Telander, M., 76
Theorizing stage, learning project, 56
Tough, A., 51, 52, 57
Turner, A., Jr., 39, 41, 43, 44, 45

Uncertainty, the power of, 14-15, 18-
19, 30-31
Undergraduate cohorts, variations among,
102-103
Unions (trade), study circles and, 87-
88, 89
United States Bureau of the Census, 74
United States Senate Special Committee
on Aging, 74-75

Verson, K., 76
Vestland, G., 94-95
Vygotsky, L. S., 7, 27-28, 29, 124

Walsh, E. J., 44
Warland, R. H., 50
Waterman, A. S., 116
Weinberg, C., 9
Whitten, N. E., Jr., 58
Williams, R. L., 7, 38-39
Wills, T. A., 16
Wolf, M. A., 76
Wolfe, A. W., 58
Wolfer, J., 15-16
Wood, J., 16
Woodside, J. H., 96
Workers' Educational Association, 86
Wright brothers' learning project, 51-59;
power variables, 57-58; stages of the,
52-56
Writing, learning and, 34, 78-79

Zeph, C. P., 69

# ORDERING INFORMATION

NEW DIRECTIONS FOR ADULT AND CONTINUING EDUCATION is a series of paperback books that explores issues of common interest to instructors, administrators, counselors, and policy makers in a broad range of adult and continuing education settings—such as colleges and universities, extension programs, businesses, the military, prisons, libraries, and museums. Books in the series are published quarterly in fall, winter, spring, and summer and are available for purchase by subscription as well as by single copy.

SUBSCRIPTIONS for 1992 cost $45.00 for individuals (a savings of 20 percent over single-copy prices) and $60.00 for institutions, agencies, and libraries. Please do not send institutional checks for personal subscriptions. Standing orders are accepted.

SINGLE COPIES cost $14.95 when payment accompanies order. (California, New Jersey, New York, and Washington, D.C., residents please include appropriate sales tax.) Billed orders will be charged postage and handling.

DISCOUNTS FOR QUANTITY ORDERS are available. Please write to the address below for information.

ALL ORDERS must include either the name of an individual or an official purchase order number. Please submit your order as follows:
*Subscriptions:* specify series and year subscription is to begin
*Single copies:* include individual title code (such as CE1)

MAIL ALL ORDERS TO:
Jossey-Bass Publishers
350 Sansome Street
San Francisco, California 94104

FOR SALES OUTSIDE OF THE UNITED STATES CONTACT:
Maxwell Macmillan International Publishing Group
866 Third Avenue
New York, New York 10022

OTHER TITLES AVAILABLE IN THE
NEW DIRECTIONS FOR ADULT AND CONTINUING EDUCATION SERIES
Ralph G. Brockett, Editor-in-Chief
Alan B. Knox, Consulting Editor